Client Case Studies
Alcoholism - Alcoholic
Practitioner Training Course
& Self Development in
Psychotherapy - Hypnotherapy
Neuro-Linguistic Programming (NLP)
Cognitive Behavioural Therapy (CBT)
Clinical Psychology Volume Three

By
David Glenn

*I am dedicating this book to my clients, in appreciation.
Thank you, because without you I would never have had the experience,
and therefore the knowledge, to write this book.
David Glenn.*

Copyright February 2017 – Revised August 2017 - David Glenn.
All rights reserved. No Unauthorized copying, distribution or use as a teaching aid.
ISBN: 9781521816349

Disclaimer, Legal Warning and Notice

THE INFORMATION ENCLOSED is for the use of the person who purchased it for reading purposes only. In spite of that, if you so wish, the knowledge can be used on yourself or clients at your own discretion. You do not have permission to resell, reprint/copy or retype any of the information enclosed, and it is not for use in teaching any classes with students. Whilst all attempts have been made to verify and check the information in this publication, neither the author, nor the publisher assumes any responsibility for errors, omissions or inaccuracies. All rights reserved. No part of this information may be reproduced or transmitted in any form, or by any means, electronically or mechanically, including, but not limited to photocopying, recording, or any form of information storage or retrieval system, without the written permission from David Glenn. This information is provided "as is" without warranty of any kind. In no event shall David Glenn be liable for any loss of profits, loss of business, loss of use of data, interruption of business, or for indirect, special, incidental, or consequential damages of any kind, arising from any error or recommendation in this material. By purchasing, or reading this book, you are agreeing and fully understand that you are responsible for your own conduct, now and in the future. The author and publisher take no liability for your actions in any way, shape or form. It is strongly advised that you do not misuse any of the techniques being taught, and we insist that you have legal insurance cover before hypnotising, or carrying therapy out on anyone.

It is with deep regret that a few past students and rival companies have attempted to copy my books and claim it as their own. Putting your name to this book as your own work, or teaching your own classes or students from it, is an infringement of copyright. I must make it clear that I take theft of my material very seriously and legal action is always taken under those circumstances. Once you have read this book and consequently gained my knowledge, I am more than happy for you to earn a good living from the information provided with clients, but not with students teaching. Please respect the years of work that I have done to produce this book and my willingness to pass my skills on to you. Under no circumstances commit a criminal act of theft against me. Due to copyright reasons I do not allow this book to be printed by you.

The CD Rom that is mentioned in this book is given to those studying as a Diploma with me personally. It is not given out for free with this book.

Contents

Disclaimer, Legal Warning and Notice......3
Introduction......6
The Workings of the Mind Model Bulletin Points......10
Alcoholic Client One Hour Fifty Minute Session......12
Pre-talk (Analytical therapy)......15
Testing your Understanding of the Knowledge......90
Seven Important Mind Rules and Mind Model......92
The End of another Volume......98

Introduction

I AM DAVID GLENN, a Professional Psychotherapist, Hypnotherapist, NLP Practitioner and Trainer with over twenty year's experience in this profession. I have written these series of books, in different volumes, to pass on my knowledge for those:

1) Interested in the cognitive psychology of oneself as a self-development help guide in understanding and utilising the power of your own mind to overcome: anxiety, depression, low confidence, phobias, stress, bad habits, weight loss, stop smoking, drugs, alcohol and more, in order to get the best out of your life. This volume is an alcoholic client case study.

2) Wanting to have a successful career in Hypnotherapy, Neuro-Linguistic Programming (NLP), Cognitive Behavioural Therapy (CBT), Life Coaching and Psychotherapy as a whole. Developing or enhancing your therapy skills in dealing with all types of clients, to help them recover their cognitive health and wellbeing.

Everybody can study this course book as home study training. This book is laid out in layman's terms, so those with no previous knowledge of the subject, can still learn how to use the power of their own mind to enrich their life. Even if you do not want to be a Professional Therapist, you can still study this course to understand yourself more, for self-help and personal development. This will enable you to break negative habits, and have unlimited confidence with the techniques that you can learn and use in your life, or therapy practice to improve your psyche, or that of a client's cognitive health (psychological health) and wellbeing.

Enrich your knowledge and skills with what I am going to teach you, which can be used in general life, for yourself and others, or by those wishing a new profession in Hypnotherapy, CBT, NLP Practitioner or Psychotherapist. Keep an open mind to new possibilities. How you have thought, communicated, and acted throughout life, may need to change, or be adapted for positive effect. I will teach you the tools of how this can be done to enable you or others to move on positively in life.

Once you have read and fully understood this book, for many people it is a life changing experience. My philosophy on therapy and psychology in general is - it is the art of understanding the psychology of people, our behaviour, the mind model, body language, communication and speech. You will be able to understand how your mind works, and how to utilise its power for positive change.

Anyone on earth, if able bodied, can drive, or learn to drive a car. Be that as it may, that does not mean you will ever be a professional rally, or formula one racing car driver. In order to be the formula one expert in the psychotherapy world, you have to have that special something: innate quality. You cannot think, act, or communicate as the general public do. In general life, what you think is rude, morally wrong, or what you would not dream of saying to a fellow human being in public, those same rules do not apply in the therapy room, because the client is paying you for a highly skilled service. You must never allow your own personality to affect what needs to be done, in order to help the client progress forwards positively in their lives. Conducting therapy is not about you or your beliefs; it is about what is best for your client: even if you have to be cruel to be kind, and go outside of your comfort zone. You may have thought that therapy is just about counselling, empathy, listening, understanding, relating to, comforting and simply relaxing a person. It is far more complex than that. You are not there to comfort a client; you are there to enable them to become unstuck, get out from their negative mindset, and move forward for positive effect and self-fulfilment. You are there to enable them to see the wood from the trees, so they can find the truth about themselves. Thereby you can support them with education, by imparting psychotherapy knowledge that can be adapted, to enable growth and movement. You will understand this more as you learn, by reading through this book in full.

I have met many students that have all the knowledge they require to be great Psychotherapist, Hypnotherapist, CBT, NLP therapist, but yet many lack intuition. This is a skill that you either already have, or you have not. Without it, success as a psychotherapist will be limited. Of course I have also met many students that have no confidence whatsoever, and I watch them grow and develop into great therapists through the knowledge from my training.

I have a very modern approach to therapy for today's generation, as I am sure you will come to realise as we continue. Once you have absorbed all the knowledge I am about to teach you, you will know more than most therapists that have been in the profession for many years.

This book contains valuable information on becoming a Prof-essional Hypnotherapist, and Psychotherapist. I will, in the greatest of detail, educate you in all aspects of NLP, CBT, Hypnotherapy and Psychotherapy, at an advanced level when working with a cannabis client.

Conducting psychotherapy is an extremely complex and skilful job. For that reason after reading this book, and gaining some practical skills, if you do not feel you have the ability to put in place the knowledge I have imparted in this book, then I will teach you the skills in a group or one on one setting. Through tailor-made training this will enable you to set up in business, with the greatest confidence in knowledge and skills to succeed in a successful psychotherapy career.

Prepare yourself for a truly amazing, life-changing experience. Enjoy as you learn, and I guarantee, at times you will be thinking: WOW! MIND BLOWING, INSPIRATIONAL KNOWLEDGE AND WISDOM, ALL IN THIS BOOK!

My recommendation is to read this book, in its entirety, more than once, to fully understand the connection between each skill being used. Please do not speed read this book, or skip pages. Take your time to absorb all the information being taught from this full real client session.

It will also be most beneficial to put the knowledge and skills into practise, by attending my group training workshop sessions or one to one training.

Dear student, it is very important, and I strongly advise that before you read this 'Volume Three' book, you first must read my book: 'Beginner to Advanced Practitioner Training Course & Self Development in Psychotherapy - Hypnotherapy - Neuro-Linguistic Programming (NLP) - Cognitive Behavioural Therapy (CBT) Clinical Psychology Vol: 1' and also 'Volume Two'. Those students that don't first read the first two volumes will lack the full understanding of this book, and as a result they will misunderstand and judge the information wrongly. Also those therapists that lack the skills, experience and confidence that I have, may also judge my way of conducting therapy wrongly if they don't first read the other volumes of this training course. I write that because the less experienced therapists that lack the skills needed to be therapist have told me that they could not conduct therapy the way that I do.

Their reason is because it is outside of their comfort zone. Even so, the facts speak for themselves. I get long-term results and they do not, and I achieve most of the successes with clients in just one session.

'Volume One' taught you in detail on how to conduct therapy, and how therapy works from a psychological point of view of understanding and changing your client's behaviour via their subconscious mind. I explained different techniques in detail, and numerous ways of conducting therapy etc, and the book was written from beginner to advanced. This book is different as was 'volume two' because I have written in full detail, word for word dialogue of what was said from a recording that I had made of a real client in a session. The recording was made just two weeks before I started to write this book. My client is more than happy for me to use the recorded dialog as a written book in order to help others. So this book is a real client case study with each book that follows being a different client case study. All personal information of my client has been changed in order to protect my client's identity i.e. their name and family information.

This book continues to grow your knowledge and skills that I have taught you in 'Volume One and Two', in a real practical client case study.

In the last two volumes I have gone into great detail to explain the techniques that I use with my clients, as such you don't need to be taught them again, or have them explained in full detail in this book. I want to avoid repeating what I have already covered in previous volumes were possible. So in this volume three, I shall simply point out what techniques I was using with this client, and when needed I will briefly explain what my intentions were with my client. You know enough by now to know the details of each technique. It is therefore very important that you read volumes one and two before reading this third volume as I have already advised.

This session with my client was conducted at an advanced level because that is how I conduct sessions, so on account of that this, once again this book is for students that have already read the first two volumes.

Throughout this book I will be giving you self-test, as I did in previous volumes with questions that challenge you to think for yourself before I reveal the answers. I do this because it is a good way for you to learn and evaluate yourself of your growing skills and knowledge.

Please remember that this is not an English literature course book, and dialogue with my client is not always grammatically correct. People have different dialects and accents.

As such, the spoken word between my client and me, as written dialogue is not always grammatically correct. This book is written word for word, what has been said between my client and me from a real therapy session. I am not going to change the spoken words in this book just to have the correct grammar. This is real life in the therapy room. This is not a novel. I am not applying for an award in English literature. I am after all a therapist, simply wanting to pass on my skills and knowledge onto you. Also I am not a professional writer.

Bear in mind that a professional writer could not have written any of my therapy books. Only me as a skilled experienced therapist can have written these books to pass on my skills and knowledge, so please consider that fact when reading.

The Workings of the Mind Model Bulletin Points

AS A STUDENT YOU must learn the mind model, and memorise it so that you can explain the knowledge to your client.

There are three recognised parts of the whole mind, even so, those that have read 'Volume One' will know my thoughts on further parts of the human mind.

There are seven mind rules in which I explained in detail in 'Volume One', and I will also add them in this book for your reference, due to their importance. There are also four reference points, so please allow me to remind you via these bulletin points.

Three parts of the whole mind:

1) Conscious Mind Functions: Rational logical thought - Makes decisions, but the subconscious determines on whether those decisions are carried out or not - One task at once - Willpower - General speech.

2) Subconscious Mind Functions: Many tasks at once - Memories - Imagination - Emotions - Habits - Protects us - In control - Intelligence - Perception of reality - Habitual speech.

3) Analytical or Critical Area: This part of the mind is the conduit connection between the conscious and subconscious, passing information between the two main parts of the whole mind. It is the part of the mind that reasons to determine new information as being fact or fiction (real or fake), based on information from the subconscious memories.

The subconscious four reference points:

A) The subconscious mind does not know the difference between what is real or imagined.
B) The subconscious also does not know the difference between good habits, or bad habits, a habit is a habit through repetition regardless.
C) The subconscious has no concept of time, past, present or future with regards to associated links.
D) The subconscious also works via associated links which are memories, cognitive thought (Fact or fiction, real or fake, true or false-truth) and emotions (Pain or pleasure) that are associated (Connected) within the mind to an anchor, which can be any sound, touch, taste, smell, or seeing a certain person (Or behaviour), colour, object or place.

The seven mind rules:

1) Ideas or thoughts result in physical immediate emotional reactions.
2) The subconscious mind delivers what we focus on.
3) Repeated negative or positive focused thoughts result in long-term organic change over-time.
4) Imagination overpowers knowledge within in the mind.
5) Fixed thoughts can only be replaced by another via the subconscious.
6) Opposing ideas cannot be held at the same time.
7) Conscious effort alone, results in opposite subconscious success.

Alcoholic Client One Hour Fifty Minute Session

DEAR STUDENT, this client is a female aged thirty seven and she believes she is addicted to the substance of Alcohol. Even so, those of you that have read the course book 'Volume One', will agree that she is wrong. This is because clients with the bad habit of drinking have wrongly associated a false-truth of pleasure, and that of being addicted to alcohol. They wrongly believe that this is a substance addiction when in fact it is mainly a psychological addiction.

Please remember that clients with bad habits have associated deluded pleasure to the psychological addiction, and neurological pain to not doing the habit, and that is partly why they do it. They also self-harm with destructive bad habits to punish themselves due to guilt, or to have a deluded sense of control over their own life that is out of control. This again is a false-truth of justification for the self-harming, and this client is a classic example of this, as you will soon become aware of as you read the session as a whole.

This client case study client is already in pain from the after effects of drinking, both neurologically (depression, stress etc) and in ill health as a direct result of her bad habit. As such it is important that I use that pain, which she is already suffering from, to change my client's associated link from pleasure to drinking, to neurological pain to the same anchor. And pleasure to not drinking alcohol instead of feelings of neurological pain. This is of course the 'Pain or pleasure technique'. This way my client will be happy to avoid the bad habit. Of course there is a lot more involved in changing my client than just using the 'Pain or pleasure technique', so it is important that I educate my client, and use a combination of many different techniques, and as a result the session will be a success. More on this in a moment as a self-test.

Those therapists that take a soft approach with clients that have bad habits fail every time long-term. How I conduct therapy takes great skill, confidence and experience, and I trust that those students that have read 'Volume One and Two' will agree with me.

This client came for a session with me after her brother had read 'volume one' of my series of books. He was impressed with what he had read, and the knowledge from the book had helped him personally. As a result he felt that I was the therapist to help his alcoholic sister. The following shown are emails from my client's brother. They are the first contact I had received from him:

First email: 'I am sending this email to see if you be able to help my sister, or help me in the right direction. She is an alcoholic who has lost her house and is in denial, when she is drunk she says that she is sober. She is 37 years old. At present she is living with our mum, who is 75 and can't cope. I am currently reading your book so I know that with her conscious mind she won't change. So she needs her subconscious mind to switch her thoughts from thinking it is a good habit to a bad one. As I said I have read your book and have changed myself but I am too close to my sister to help her. Can you help with this situation at all?'

Second email: 'Just a few things that might help. We lost our dad 8 years ago and when she is drunk she blames herself. She has lost her house from spending her money on drink and her children who are 13 and 12 don't want anything to do with her. She did have a good job but she got arrested for drink driving so ended up losing her job. Basically she is at rock bottom but doesn't realise it. After putting all this down now it seems more than a session for alcoholism alone.'

Dear student, what was written in the first email is correct, his sister does need to switch her thoughts from thinking that alcohol is a good habit (neurological pleasure) to a bad habit (neurological pain) on a subconscious level. However by simply associating neurological pain to the habit, that alone will not help this client to stop abusing herself with drink.

As my student this is your first self-test. Can you think as to why the 'Pain and Pleasure technique' when used on its own will not change this client's destructive pattern of behaviour long-term? In other words I am asking you, what do I need to do to permanently change my client's behaviour other than by just using the 'Pain and Pleasure' technique? Please think about that before reading on.

The reason that the 'Pain and Pleasure technique' alone with not save this client is because by just dealing with the effect (alcoholism) does not change the event-cause, or her perception of the event-cause of her alcoholism. Remember that it is very important as a good therapist to remember 'cause and effect'. Most therapist, and all doctors just deal with the effects that is drinking, and the secondary effects of depression, stress and ill health etc. By doing so the event-cause, or perception of it that led to the effects remains. As such so does all of the effects of alcoholism, those being psychological and physical ill health. This is why it was very important that I dealt with this client's main event-cause to her effects. The possible event-cause was revealed in her brother's emails, which is the emotional blame this client feels from the death of their dad. If I can't change the cause then I must change my client's perception of the event-cause, and by doing so the effects are removed, those being drinking, depression, stress, self-blame etc. This will save her life.

Dear student, before we begin walking through the session in detail, I feel that it is important to remind you of the following:

When I asked my client questions, I was leading her to consciously think of answers. By doing so I was creating a 'Trans-Derivational Search (TDS)' within her mind. As I explained in 'Volume One', a 'Trans-Derivational Search (TDS)', is a type of everyday trance state, and often a state of internal lack of certainty or openness to finding an answer. TDS is a fundamental part of human language and cognitive processing. Arguably, every word or utterance a person hears, and everything they see or feel and take note of, results in a very brief trance while TDS is being carried out to establish a contextual meaning for it.

At the point of being asked a question, since something is being checked out at that moment consciously within her mind, it can be utilised in order to create, or to continue a trance state. In the pre-talk this state is a mild to light trance state, which as a result also eliminates the 'Fight or Flight Response' by relaxing my client when with me. My client's conscious mind is effectively sent on a journey of trying to find the answers to my questions. This is the bypassing of my client's conscious mind (TDS), which also opens up her subconscious to my suggestions. As such I could continue to lead her, with suggested statements, and leading answers to my questions, which seeped into her unguarded subconscious as fact, because she had no conscious guard due to the conscious bypass (TDS).

For those reasons throughout the session I created many 'Trans-Derivational Searches (TDS)' within my client's conscious mind. This allowed me to remain in control of my clients thought processes and by extension the session as a whole.

In this session I felt that educating my client was a priority to change her perception of reality [of the main event-cause] whilst in a light trance. This was the reason I did not use a deeper level of hypnosis, plus I wanted her to communicate with me verbally throughout the session, so no hypnotic induction was used with this client. Also she understood me, and I noticed a positive change in her, so there was no need for a hypnotic deep induction to be used within this session. More on this throughout the explanation of this session.

Pre-talk (Analytical therapy)

Dear student, let us begin. My client arrived for therapy with her caring brother and she sat down. I gave her the option of her brother remaining throughout the session, or the alternative of having a private session with me without him being present. Even though her brother knows all that there is to know about her, both were happy for the session to be conducted one on one, so her brother left the room. By giving my client an option of her whether her brother remained in the room or not, gave my client a sense of control. This of course helped her to relax in my presence. The first TDS had taken place for the benefit of my client and me. The following was then said by me to my client:

> Me: "Right, Amy. You are thirty seven?"
> Client replied in a confident tone, "Yeah."
> Me: "So why are you here?"
> Client: "Erm...basically erm... I've just been like very distressed recently. Drinking more..... Erm..... Not sleeping, not eating, just basically really.... tense. I have tried therapy..... Erm... I have got an appointment to see my alcohol worker again tomorrow because my alcohol level has gone up again. And my brother just thought try something else."

Dear student, did you notice the leading 'Yes Set Question' which provoked compliance from my client? That being: 'You are thirty seven?' I obviously already knew the answer as it was said in my question, so my clients led reply was in agreement with me. This builds rapport. Simple, subtle and highly affective.

My next question was: "So why are you here?" Again I already knew the answer but this time the question was an 'Open-ended Question' to allow my client the opportunity talk to me in detail.

My clients reply made it known to me that she has been having counselling, and it simply has not worked because she is still drinking. You know my thoughts on councillors having read 'volume one', they have no idea what they are doing, and I could tell you many horror stories. As a result of her counsellors failure to help her, her new approach, thanks to her brother reading one of my books, is to seek help from me a psychotherapist.

Dear student, I will share with you the following: A man that I know who is a friend of a friend, was seeing a counsellor and still is. He has multiple extreme issues of chronic depression, stress, anxiety, low self-esteem and a warped sense of reality. He gets upset over nothing at all. He wants constant attention of affection of love, and he is overly clingy towards the people around him. This is due to the loss of his mother as a young child. The best way of describing him is that he is a baby in an adult's body. He lacks understanding of himself and the world around him. As such his reactions to situations are simply odd and uncomfortable to the people he meets. He had personally done me a favour in which I paid him for even though he had not asked me for any money. Even so he was thankful for the money. I was friendly towards him as I am with everyone. And even though he had never had a therapy session with me, I would help him to understand himself, the mind model, reality etc. This he enjoyed and found very helpful, and I did see a positive change within him. Regardless, I was never affectionate towards him, and I did not contact him every day because there was no need to do so. He isn't a close friend. Regardless, he told his counsellor that he thought I was very selfish because I was not contacting him each and every day. Instead of his counsellor explaining to him that the relationship between him and I was nothing more than acquaintance, that as such did not warrant daily contact, the counsellor agreed with him that I was selfish. His councillors response in agreement with him had done nothing more than wrongly justify his negative way of thinking. This validation of his negative warped realty undid all the good work I had helped him achieve. As a good therapist you never defend a destructive negative thought, never reinforce a warped negative perception of reality, but that is what the counsellor had done. As a result he isolated himself from society for many month and was suicidal.

Let us now carry on with the client case study session.

I continued with another 'Open-ended Question' by saying: "What therapy have you tried?"

Client: "Erm I have had counselling. One to one counselling with 'Relate' and erm…..something else….CBT."

Me: "And how have you found that?" Meaning what were the results and her thoughts on her previous therapy.

Client: "Erm…. It works in the short term. Erm… counselling I found really good. I did like the first twelve sessions, and then she said to me do you want to carry on, you know you can have some more sessions. And I said yeah because… I felt a lot of things that I couldn't tell other people….. I could. I was in this room, this woman didn't know me from Adam and I could tell her anything. You know, even if was only what I had done that week… rather than—you know, and then other deep things as well."

Me: "Did they use hypnosis?"

Client: "No."

Me: "As regards CBT what have you done there?"

Client: "Erm… that was more like mindfulness. You know like trying to relax. Erm…. Wasn't really hypnotherapy but she did recommend some like listening to things as I went to sleep. You know just like calming music and things like that. I did try that and that helped. But like I say the thing is with me is… I kind of think I'm ok now so I stop it and really I should keep it there so in times of stress, go back to those techniques."

Me: "Right Okay," Then in an excitable tone to provoke an association of pleasure I said, "Yeah because this is a lifelong thing—"

Mirroring me in a high almost excitable tone my client replied: "Yeah."

Dear student, this mirroring from my client told me that she was highly suggestable, which is great in therapy but not so great in life in general if surrounded by negativity.

My client, previous to seeing me, had twelve sessions with a councillor as she had stated. Clearly that councillor has failed. Too many so called therapist claim to be using CBT when they do not even know what it is. CBT as you know is 'Cognitive behavioural therapy'. It is about educating a client on their cognitive thoughts, and behaviour that is controlled from their emotions via their imagination, or perception of a given situation. And CBT is about teaching clients how to change. CBT is not about just listening to a client over twelve sessions.

At this point of the session after just two minutes, I already knew that my client felt comfortable in my presence. I knew this because she was mirroring my tone of voice. As a result the rapport was already strong between Amy and me. This was partly achieved by my calm relaxed easy going nature which had put my client at ease, which of course helped in the removal of the 'Fight or Flight Response'. Not only that, my client had gain a belief and trust in me previous to meeting me, due to her brother having read my 'volume one' book. He had obviously conveyed his belief in me to his sister, and that was a huge help in the success of this session.

With the use of an analogy to what my client had said, I continued: "It is like you wouldn't stop eating healthily all of a sudden—" (Leading Yes Set or Influenced thought technique due to the words, 'you wouldn't stop')

Client: "Yeah," said in a positive agreeable, in an almost excitable tone.

I continued my sentence: "And start eating crap…. And then expect to have the same body—"

Client: "Yeah."

Me: "From eating healthy—" (Leading Yes Set or Influenced thought technique)

Client: "Yeah."

Me: "Throughout life you have got to look after your body." (Leading Yes Set or Influenced thought technique)

Client: "Yeah."

Me: "If you don't then it isn't going to look after you." (Leading Yes Set or Influenced thought technique) (Mild neurological pain)
Client: "Yeah."

Dear student, when a client interrupts the therapist sentences, as long as the interruptions are positive in agreement then it is perfectly fine. In fact it is a good indication of a strong rapport connection as she clearly felt comfortable enough to interrupt in a positive agreeable tone. At this point, to this part of the session, my client and I were in a common reality due to the agreement of what I had said so far. The use of 'Yes set' leading verbal psychology was, and continued to be throughout the session, very influential with my clients thoughts. That played a large part in gaining rapport due to the led agreement from my client.

The mild neurological pain was added to test my client response. She had responded well so I knew I could grow a stronger sense of neurological pain associated to her habit, and to not stopping the habit over the course of this session.

I continued: "Right, has anybody ever educated you on your mind (Mind model), on your state of mind, and your situation?" I already knew the answer would be no.

Client: "Nobody has but I have read books, and you know like I say about mindfulness and things I can relate to, and use some of those techniques... You know just like...like erm... I had a row with my mum the other day and I went and stayed at a friends for two days. So I was dreading going home. So I was using the mindfulness of right – when I go in the morning, right this is what I am doing this morning... don't think about that until you get to that point. You know rather than all day thinking I've got to go and see my mum and all of that. So just using— Right this is what I am doing now, let's concentrate on this, right that is what I am doing then. Then we get onto that you know."

Me: "Living the moment—"
Client: "Yeah."
Me: "Instead—"

Dear student, I didn't need to finish my sentence off by saying, 'Instead....of thinking about the dread of going home in the morning'. This is because my client had already said it so my use of the word 'instead' was in agreement of her previous sentence, and then my client agreed with me.

Client: "Yeah."

Dear student, my client had read phycology books but not my books. The books she has read had simply not taught her what she needed to know, or she has misinterpreted them. I know this because her version of mindfulness techniques have simply not worked for her. Allow me to explain in detail. After a row with her mum she had ran away for two days instead of changing her mindset to a positive one to remain at home. She was dreading the thought of going back home, as a consequence of clearly not using a technique correctly to overcome that negative mindset regardless of her thoughts that she had done.

I know this because the night before going back home she had been thinking, 'When I go [home] in the morning, right this is what I am doing this morning... don't think about that until you get to that point'. What she had said was a 'Conflicting statement', and as such a contradiction to what she wanted to achieve. Remember the analogy of, 'Don't think about a black cat' from 'volume one'. Well you achieve the opposite and think about a black cat. That is what my client had done. She had been overly thinking of what she needed to do in the morning, that of going home. And then she had thought not to think about it. By doing so she was thinking about it, and that is why she dreading to go home. She had been imagining a negative scenario of returning home. She then added to her confusion by thinking of two moments at the same time. She had said, '(First moment) Right this is what I am doing now, let's concentrate on this, (Second moment) right that is what I am doing then'. The 'then' was the act of going home. That was the complete opposite of what she didn't want to think about. She had created her own anxiety by imagining a negative outcome. That imagined thought had affected her emotional state which in turn had affected her behaviour, and that limited her ability to think [consciously] logically.

My client needed to be educated, and she needed to understand fully. Even so, I had to avoid confrontation, and I didn't want to overwhelm my client all at once, so there was no point, at this stage of the session, in sharing with her all of the information I have just divulged to you my student. Small steps are needed to change her mindset over the course of this session.

I continued: "So how long have you been drinking for?"

Client: "Erm about," with a noticeable outtake of breath in contempt of her own situation she continued, "Six years."

Me: "And what triggered the drinking?" Of course I already knew the answer, even so it was important that my client tells me. This is because it would be yet another good indication that she is comfortable in my presence and that she is ready for positive change.

Without hesitation my client said: "Well my dad died nearly nine years ago, and I was coping for a long time and then just—I don't know what happened.....but suddenly I started having these recurring dreams of the day he got poorly, and the whole process, and it was every night.... And I wasn't sleeping, and I was getting up and you know like pouring myself a glass of wine to try and chill out, and it just like kind of increased and increased..... And I just got into a habit really...."

Me: "So you used wine to disassociate yourself"

Dear student, this had not been a 'Closed-ended Question', it was an led 'Influenced thought technique' because no choice of 'yes' or 'no' was given as a reply. This is because of the way I had verbalised the rhetorical question. It was said in an authoritarian way of, 'So you...' and not, 'Had you...'. The result was that my client was led to agree, as if it was her original thought that she had used wine to disassociate yourself from the grief of her dad's death. In agreement I had avoided confrontation and had compounded rapport with my client.

Also note that my client had said in relation to the aftermath of her dad's death, "I was coping for a long time", the fact is she had been suppressing her grief within her mind for a long time, and by doing so the neurological pain had been building which had then had a greater negative impact on her. Suppressing grief is not the solution to overcoming grief. Crying is not a sign of weakness. It is natural and healthy to cry in order to release the pain to be able to move forwards in life.

Client: "Yeah," led agreement due to the 'Influenced thought technique' as previously described, "and then I moved onto like hard things like Rocka."

I had never heard of Rocka so I asked: "So you started to take drugs?"

Client: "No I'm not taking any drugs."

Me: "What is Rocka?"

Client: "Vodka! Sorry."

Me: "Oh Vodka, I thought you said Rocka."

My client laughed and said: "Sorry I am a bit stuffy." The fact that she had laughed was a great sign that I could built associations of pleasure later in the session to not drinking.

Me: "Okay. So would you class yourself as an alcoholic?" (Closed-ended Question.)

Client: "Yeah."

Me: "Yeah....." I took down some written notes to what had been said and then I continued, "Would you class yourself as a self-abuser?"

Client: "Yeah."

Me: "Yeah..... Have you read my book?"

Client: "No"

Me: "Have you seen my book?"

Client: "No."

I said, whilst pointing at a stack of my books to influence my client to look at them, "That is my book. Your brother has read my book, and that is the reason you are here....." I had pointed out my books to add more credibly to my experience and knowledge within my clients mind. I continued, "Right what are you angry about?"

My client once again had a noticeable outtake of breath of contempt towards her own self-abuse when she replied: "Just the way.... I've....I've behaved, and I have ruined....so much of my life and....people around me and....I am angry at myself that I know I have done it, but yeah I am still doing it."

Me: "And why are you still doing it?"

Client: "Because it is like a vicious cycle....I am angry with myself, I get stressed....and like have a drink, or I have self-harmed in the past... to try and like calm myself down. I have always had very low self-esteem. And I find it very hard when people compliment me....I can't believe it."

Dear student, when a person self-abuses in anyway, they do so because they are venting their angry, or guilt from a situation that they have caused, or another person has caused. The self-abuser wrongly believes the situation is out of their control, and as a negative consequence the self-abuse in all cases, included my client's case, gives the self-abuser a deluded sense of control over their life that was wrongly perceived as being out of control. The act of self-abuse also disassociates them from dealing with the event-cause, but this suppression doesn't last because in time it overwhelms the self-abuser and they suffer chronic stress and depression. This then makes it impossible for them to help themselves out of the bad situation.

I had asked my client the question, 'Right what are you angry about?' The answer I was given was not the main event-cause of her anger. This is because what my client had described was her own anger towards herself from the effect of drinking, and not the anger from the main event-cause that had led her to drinking. Basically her anger as described was a secondary-effect from the first-effect of drinking, and not anger from the main event-cause, which is her dad's death, to drinking (first-effect). This is very important to recognise as a therapist. The main event-cause, and first and second-effects from the event-cause must be understood. As a therapist you wouldn't want to confuse a first-effect as the main event-cause, or a secondary-effect as the event-cause to drinking, or anger because then the correct main event-cause would not be dealt with, and so the negative effects would continue. We already know that the main event-cause was this client's dad's death. Even so, at this point of the session I still did not know the full main event-cause situation surrounding his death, and as such, obviously I wanted my client to delve deeper into the main event-cause situation. I did this without the need of asking her directly about the full true main event-cause in order to allow my client to divulge in her own comfortable time. Never rush a client because it is important to avoid associations of discomfort of them communicating with you their therapist.

I continued to compound rapport when saying: "We all have low self-esteem to a certain degree and we all....we all go within ourselves when we receive a compliment. Everybody is the same there. Different levels, but we are all the same there." I then asked: "Right so.... What are you punishing yourself for?

Dear student, the question of: 'What are you punishing yourself for?' is the same leading type of question as 'Right what are you angry about?' I was leading my client to abreact to release the pain by allowing her to open up about the true event-cause without being direct about her dad's death. I had avoided being direct at this early stage of the session. The question is very leading because it makes my client aware (indirectly) that I am not fully satisfied with her reply to my other leading question of, 'Right what are you angry about?' I had made it clear to my client indirectly that I wanted her to expand on the information without having to be direct about her dad's death, the event-cause.

After eight minutes of the session, with emotion in her voice for the first time, my client replied: "Because I don't really.......I don't really like myself...."

Dear student, my clients reply had again been in relation to a secondary-effect and not the event-cause, as such I continued with leading indirect questions.

Me: "And what do you not like about yourself?"
Client: "Erm...All of it like my life...Erm like me.... and what I be.....erm... I just... I don't feel worthy... of things."

Dear student, again her reply had been about secondary-effects, so I continued to lead to get the whole truth of the event-cause situation.

Me: "But why?
Client: "Because I have done a lot of bad things. You know I was a horrible teenager, in trouble......in trouble with the police and you know I've done a lot of bad things."

Dear student, my clients last spoken sentences where in relation to an event-cause to feeling guilty, but not the event-cause to her drinking or secondary-effects from that. My client was suppressing the full details of the more recent event-cause due to her strong neurological pain associated to it. As a result she had gone further back in time to events that were not having the greater negative impact on her. The information from my client was good but her suppression of the more powerful event-cause was not healthy for her. She had tried to please me, and distract me from the true event-cause by giving me an event-cause of lesser impact. I knew this so I continued to lead my client to the true event-cause without being direct, so as to allow her time to remain comfortable in divulging the full details of the main event-cause.

Skilful and complex conducting therapy is it. You must have the skills and patience of a saint.

I continued: "And what have you done?"
Client: "Erm I have been done for drink driving and that is why my brother drives me. Erm….."
Me: "Have you lost your driving license?" (Yes Set Question)
Client: "Yeah. I can get it back now. But erm….because I couldn't drive and erm….I lost my job and….it's all through me…. just really being….a bit selfish and just—but not in a way of going out having fun. I just….don't know…I just….I can't really describe it. I just don't…don't—" (All secondary-effects and not them main event-cause)
Me: "You are lost in a fog."
Uplifting her tone due to my understanding analogy of the fog, my client replied: "Yeah! Yeah" basically yeah that's it I am just like….."
Me: "You are in a rut and you don't know how to get out of it."
Client: "Yeah"
Me: "Because you are in a vicious cycle. What else have you lost?"
Client: "Erm…." In an emotional tone my client upsettingly replied, "My boyfriend….and he stuck by me for a long time when…I was… you know, when I was really low and I was….."
Me: "You can't expect anyone to stay around forever, even family."
Client: "I know, I know."
Me: "At some point they have had enough."
Client: "That is it, I have lost a lot of friends….through it as well."
Me: "What else have you lost?"

Dear student, these questions of loss are to provoke an abreaction of negative pain that I can then associate to her bad drinking habit. Her replies were all first and secondary-effects and not the full details of the event-cause. However the information given is good as I was leading her to open up about the main event-cause.

Client: "Erm...I haven't really lost my children, but they live with their dad now. I do see them. You know, it's not like they have been taken away from me or anything. But I've lost... the relationship I use to have with them...."

Me: ""Do they enjoy seeing you?

Client: "Yes and no because.... You know some days..... I am up and erm I can be like fine, and then other days I just don't want to get out of bed, and I'm like...."

Changing the subject to a positive, I said: "What is the longest you have been without a drink?"

Client: "Erm... I was clean for eight months when I was in the erm... alcohol program last time...."

Me: "How long ago was that?"

Client: "That was about two years ago...."

Me: "And how did you feel in that time?"

In an upbeat tone my client replied: "Really good... and now when erm.... I don't have a drink for a few days, I'm like looking after myself you know. Getting up, having a wash, going out, doing things. I felt a lot better, but then the slightest thing, and at the moment it's my mum because she doesn't understand....like I shouldn't and....anxiety.... and you know sometimes certain things will get me anxious.... and I get like quite tense and agitated....and... that's when I think right, if I can just have a drink I can calm down and deal with this.... But... erm... like mum... it hit a point last night when she was like well you have done everything. She said, 'What's the point in trying anything else because you will just fail at that...' And it's little put downs like that that makes me think – why should I... you know."

Me: "So she hasn't helped you at all?"

Client: "No."

Me: "Right well let's ignore her. Certain things that get you stressed, what gets you anxious and stressed?"

Dear student, I underlined 'Certain things that get', to bring to your attention that I had said those words to mirror what my client had previously said. This continues to compound rapport in agreement.

Client: "Erm... new situations.... Erm....."

Me: "Fear of the unknown?" said because a new situation is an unknown.

Client: "Yeah... erm.... Talking about myself.... Meeting new people...."

I continued: "Okay. Is there anything you feel guilty about?" Another leading question without being direct in associating the question to the main event-cause.

Client: "Yeah..." with a noticeable upsetting tone in her voice she said, "My dad's death...." (Main event-cause)

Me: "That is what I was waiting for...." In a calm empathising tone I asked, "Why do you feel guilty?"

Dear student, as the session continued, my client revealed the full truth of the main event-cause of her self-abuse, anger, guilt etc. Before reading her continued dialog I wish to bring to your attention the following: From the last several spoken dialogue's, that you have just read that had been spoken by me to my client, have you noticed how I adapted my indirect leading questions to her main event-cause without being direct about the cause? Please allow me to remind you that the questions asked to my client, were not directly associated to the main event-cause because I wanted her guard 'Fight or Flight Response' to remain down in order to give my client time, in her own comfortable time, to divulge the details of her deepest personal trauma that is her main event-cause.

What I had not done, was allow my client to lead me away from the main event-cause to a more distant event-cause from her teenage years. I had not focused on the path that she had tried to lead me down. I had not allowed her to continue in suppressing the main event-cause. Instead I had patiently indirectly led her to reveal the full story of the main event-cause to her problems. As a result she remained comfortable in being open to talk to me more. All this patience of skilful indirect leading had led to the point of my client telling me the following in relation to the main event-cause.

Client: "....Because erm... I was supposed to take him to the hospital for a routine appointment on the Monday. But he already hurt his knee... He was having an operation on that knee, and he was going for a routine appointment to have it checked. But on the Saturday before he fell and banged that knee. So when I went to pick him up on the Monday...

because mum was out playing golf." My client was sniffing with a runny noise due to feeling slightly upset, and then she continued, "Sorry I have some tissues." She looked into her bag to get a tissue to wipe her noise and then continued, "Erm... I went to get him and he erm... he said, 'I'm not going'. I said 'Why?' and he said, 'Well I can hardly walk. You know they won't miss me, and I'll probably not manage, and I am certainly not going in a wheel chair'. So he refused to go.... And then on the Tuesday he was so bad he couldn't get erm... out of his chair. He had one of those reclining chairs, you know they have got like two settees like this," She was referring to the two settees in the room that her and I where sat on, "And then one reclining chair, and he was in that with his knee up, and he couldn't get out of it so erm... He was really struggling. Mum was helping him, having to help him get to the toilet and everything... Erm...so on the Tuesday mum was talking to her friend telling her he is refusing to go to hospital, or see the doctor, and her friend said, 'Phone the emergency doctor'. And mum did. He came out and checked him over, and did some bloods and erm....That was on a Wednesday. On the Thursday morning at 8 o'clock saying that they were sending for an ambulance....because you know there is something seriously wrong with him. So mum tried... to wake him up but she couldn't. And she tried phoning me but I was driving my boyfriend at the time.... And I had my phone on silent like in the car, and anyway I dropped him off. Driving back with the kids I thought I'll just check my phone and it said like six missed calls, three voice mail, so I pressed it and my mum was like – 'Oh I can't wake your dad and there is an ambulance coming'. So I... literally run a red light and I got there and erm... You know he was in intensive care for a week and they said, 'You know if he had been seen to sooner, we could have caught it with antibiotics.'

Me: "He had a blood infection."

Dear student, I knew it was a blood infection because I had recognised the described symptoms as being the same from one of my family members, those being a blood infection that was cured with antibiotics within four days. My family member was one hundred and six years of age at the time so it is clear that my client's dad could have also been cured.

With a tonal upsetting quivering in my client's voice, she continued: "Yeah… erm… and my other brother erm… he actually said to me, 'If you had taken him [to hospital] he would still be here [alive]'. And then in anger my mum said, 'It's your fault'." Getting increasingly upset my client took a moment to blow her nose.

Me: "…. But whose fault is it really?"
Client: "No one's fault it is just….."
Me: "It is someone's fault, so whose fault is it?"
Visibly upset my client replied: "My dad's"
Me: "Yes. What has it got to do with you that he decided not to go to hospital? Your mum… and your brother are in pain, and they have got to blame somebody. That is their issue not yours. What they did was wrong, and they was wrong. It had nothing to do with you your dads death. Your dad's death was his decision. He decided not to go to the hospital. That is down on him. Nobody else but him. You were going to take him, you was willing to take him….. But he refused… so whose fault is it?"
Client: "Him."

Dear student, notice how I had led my clients thoughts to remove the guilt away from herself, within her mind, onto the true person to blame for her dads death. That person being him, her dad. I did that without being direct in telling her myself. It was very important to lead my client to say her dad instead of being directly told. The reason being is because the thought and emotional response to the thought is more powerful, and beneficial when seemingly generated within my client's subconscious mind without any influence. Class this as an 'Influenced thought technique' if you so wish.

It is also interesting to note that even if my client had said it was her mums fault, that answer would still have been led by my words because there was only two people to choose from. Remember that her mum was playing golf the day my client's dad should have gone to hospital. So her mum hadn't cared enough about her husband. Golf had been more important to her than his hospital appointment, and she had put the burden of responsibility on to her child, my client. No other people were to blame. Not my client, her brothers, or the Doctor. This is the reason my clients mum had vented her pain of abandonment guilt and sorrow onto my client by blaming her. My clients mum was trying to dissociate herself from the blame.

I continued: "What has bothered you more is your mums and brothers reaction blaming you. But that is their issues. What they did there is disgusting."

Dear student, remember to always ridicule abusers, and not self-abusers, in order to lessen their negative destructive power over a client's mind. My last spoken dialog to my client was a great example of me doing that. My client's relationship with them was bad anyway, and it is not my job to change them, or fix those relationships. My priority is my client's wellbeing, and so I am slowly making my client aware of the facts of the bad relationships, and so she never has to feel upset by their negativity again. I continue to change my client's perception of the reality of her relationships over the course of this session. You will learn more on this as you continue to read.

My client continued to express emotional hurt in her voice, and body language when saying: "I am [disgusted]… and this is where I feel guilty as well because I am cross with my dad…. for leaving me because I was very close to my dad. And that is another reason…. I am cross with him, and I feel guilty for being cross with him because he is dead."

Me: "Yeah, you are feeling guilty, and angry at him because he has let you down, and he has let himself down by not going to the hospital, and by doing that he let you down. And that has made you angry, and that is why you now abuse yourself…. All that building up from being a teenager, you was bad as a teenager… police involved and it has just been a progression of things throughout life, and your pushing point… was your dad— (Main event-cause)"

Whilst nodding her head in agreement she mumbled: "Mmmmm." This was an internal yes in agreement to what I had said.

Dear student, the following dialog I am going to explain to you in a moment. First read my spoken words as said to my client and see if you can work out what my intentions were. And what skills and techniques were being used. Let us begin:-

Me: "But that was his issue, and his decision…. He didn't care enough about himself…. to go to the hospital…. What your brother and your mum said was wrong wasn't it. Because is it actually your fault?"

Client: "No."

Me: "No..... It is not your fault at all. You couldn't cope with somebody giving you an insult and putting you down. You took it literally—"

Client: "Yeah."

I continued my previous sentence by saying "As if it is real. And it is not real. That is their perception of a situation."

Dear student, the dialog you have just read, please read it all again to test yourself on what you notice. I will now reveal the hidden skills involved, and maybe the test will also reveal what you did and didn't notice.

First I had said, "But that was his issue, and his decision.... He didn't care enough about himself.... to go to the hospital.... What your brother and your mum said was wrong wasn't it." That had been said in an authoritarian way to remove my client of the blame from her dad's decision of not going to hospital, which had contributed to his death. My dialog also disassociated my client from her mums and brothers wrong doings before I asked, "Because is it actually your fault?" My client had replied, "No."

Mirroring my clients tone I had said the same word, "No..... " Clearly said to reinforce the rapport between my client and me before the continuance in saying, "It is not your fault at all. You couldn't cope with somebody giving you an insult and putting you down. You took it literally—" My client had replied, "Yeah."

I had then continued my previous sentence by saying "As if it is real. And it is not real. That is their perception of a situation."

Dear student, had you noticed what I have just pointed out to you? If so well done. But wait a minute, surly there is more being achieved in what I had said to my client, isn't there? Well yes there is, a lot more in fact. Allow me to explain: Remember in 'volume one' when I taught you about 'verbal skills' and 'conflicting statements'. I advised you to avoid 'conflicting statements' when wanting to provoke positivity. That advice is still correct. With that being known, have you noticed the two 'conflicting statements' in my last two dialogs that I had spoken to my client? If so then once again well done. You may have noticed, but do you know why I had used 'conflicting statements' when they seem to contradict how I have taught you on how to conduct therapy? First I had said the 'conflicting statement' of, 'actually your fault' in reference to the blame of her dads death when asking, "because is it actually your fault?" And secondly I had said, 'your fault' when saying, "It is not your fault at all".

Allow me to explain why, because my use of 'conflicting statements' within this session do not go against my teachings, even though at first they may seem otherwise to students that are still learning, or therapist that lack the skills needed to be therapist.

Firstly even though it consciously seemed that I was trying to provoke positivity by making her realise that she was not at fault, I was in fact purposely creating a conflict within her mind on a subconscious level by the use of 'conflicting statements'. Are you confused as to why I would do that? I will now explain in detail. Over the many years of experience of conducting therapy I realised that I could use 'conflicting statements' to test a client's emotional level to an insult, or accusation of blame, without directly insulting them. This could also be used to educate a client, and by doing so, also change their perception of a negative given situation to an association that is beneficial for them.

In this case I had indirectly provoked the negatives in the form of 'conflicting statements' to test my client. I wanted to know if she would reflect on her past negative thoughts, before responding [or reacting], via her new external perception of a common reality, with use of her new growing knowledge, instead of just reacting via her previous negative internal perception of reality. I had wanted to know if my client could handle indirect insults, or accusations from me in the form of a 'conflicting statements'. I was testing her emotional response and behaviour to what could be seen as an insult, or pointing the finger of blame. And I was trusting that she would cope by reflecting with the use of her new knowledge (common reality viewed externally) instead of reacting badly via her previous destructive internal perception of reality. She reflected and responded very well because of her growing knowledge and change of perception, plus the fact I had first disassociated her from the blame (as previously described) before saying the first 'conflicting statement'. By conducting therapy this way my client was led to not allow the negative conflicting statements to bother her. It allows her to learn subconsciously that she can cope. And as you know, the subconscious is the most powerful part of the whole mind, and so her emotional and behavioural responses were tested, which had changed for the better because she reflected then responded in a positive rational way.

Once again in summary, remember I had used disassociation when saying, "But that was his issue, and his decision.... He didn't care enough about himself.... to go to the hospital.... What your brother and your mum said was wrong wasn't it." I had then tested my clients emotions and behavioural responses with the first 'conflicting statement' when saying, "Because is it actually your fault?" My client had passed my test by replying with a definite and confident, "No."

Before saying the second 'conflicting statement', I had reinforced the rapport between my client and me with my mirroring tone, and by the use of the word 'no' because my client had previously used the same word in her reply. This way she remained comfortable, with her guard down, and so I had been confident that she would cope with the second 'conflicting statement' as follows, "No..... It is not your fault at all".

I had continued to lead my client to have a different perception of her past given situations of insults, and as such she had, in her present tense, given a different response to the hidden insults (subliminal) to what she would have done in her past. In the past my client had reacted emotionally negatively to the insults from her mum and brother, and that emotional response had affected her behaviour to drink. But now I had changed her perception of the insults. Partly due to the use of 'confliction statements'.

In contrast I had then reminded her of her past negative emotional state by saying, "You couldn't cope (past tense) with somebody giving you an insult and putting you down." I had then started to make her aware of how unnecessary her past negative emotional reactions were by having said, "You took (past tense) it [insults] literally—". My client had then broken my sentence to agree with me, as led when saying, "Yeah." I had then continued my last sentence by saying, "As if it is real. And it is not real. That is their perception of a situation." This had led my client to realise that their perception was wrong, therefore her past conditioned perception of the situation was also wrong. This concludes that the common perception of reality, when viewed externally, is that she was never at fault. I had made her aware that her past negative emotions were led by her taking insults literally (negative internal view of reality). Alternatively when in a healthy common perception of reality, spoken words are not to be taken literally because the meaning of the words are not real. Words are only another person's perception of her from a situation which had affected her perception of herself in a negative way. All the while I had associated what I had said to being the same situation of her brothers and mums abuse towards her. This had been a fantastic way of educating my client within her subconscious without being direct in my approach. I had not directly insulted her. What a great result in a positive direction. Would you have ever thought that 'conflicting statements' could be used for such a positive result. How fantastic was that.

Now let us continue with the session.

In reference to her mum and brother, I said, "They have got to blame somebody. When somebody is in pain, when someone is hurt, that pain has got to be projected somewhere. Both, either project that pain onto themselves by self-harming, or they project the pain onto somebody else. Your mum and your brother projected that pain away from themselves onto you, and then you projected your pain onto yourself by abusing yourself."

Dear student, do you see how I had simplified my clients situation. What she had previous to the session seen as overwhelming, and therefore a difficult vast task to understand and overcome, I had changed that negative confused perception of the same situation to being simple to understand, and as such easy to overcome. This simple change of perception of her reality continues throughout the session as we continue.

Also notice that as I was educating her, building on her new knowledge, I would repeat previously said information in order to lead her to continue to reflect on her past via her growing knowledge from her new external view of reality. This is why as a therapist you must repeat to your client, because repetition seeps deep within the client's subconscious for positive lifelong results.

Some students, and people that have read my books have complained about the repetition. Those people lack understand of the importance of repeating information to a client, as just described because they don't read in detail the books. They instead flick through speed reading, and then comment without realising the true skill involved in conducting therapy. Plus the fact that repetition is the mother of successes in changing a person's mindset on a subconscious level, and as a result their emotional and behavioural responses for the better in any given situation. You will notice this repetition more throughout this client case study, even so I always, were needed, change the way I verbalise the same information to a client in order to keep them interested.

Continuing with the session, my client spoke normally as if the burden of pain had been lifted from her when she said: "Yeah that's it, because like I say... two years... I was fine you know ... I was coping and everyone kept saying to me you know. And everyone was coming to me.... I've always been that kind of person that everyone comes to me, but like I say I am very, very private person, so if I have got a problem... I just keep it here. I don't go to anybody."

Me: "But you have done. And that is what you needed to release it. Right! So.... What you did as a teenager is completely irrelevant now. You was a teenager... a teenage rebel... so that is the past. You have no police record now because of it, it gets removed and that's the past. Is there anything that you feel guilty about there?"

Client: "......No just.... Just like you say it is the past and I can't change that now...."

Dear student, remember that I had previously not allowed my client to focus the direction of the session on to an irrelevant distant event-cause from her teenage years. I had now made my client fully aware that this session was not going in that direction, and as led my client had agreed with me. Once again, a fantastic result so that I could deal with the true main event-cause. This is an example of the importance of a therapist keeping control of the overall session and direction. This requires skill and experience. Let's continue:

Me: "What you can do is change your perception of it. You was young. You was naive. You was vulnerable. You was easily led... by other people."

Client: "Well yeah I ended up getting off because mum and dad were not around very much when I was a teenager and Ken.... Ken brought me up quite a bit. Erm...."

Me: "You have got two brother then." (Yes Set Question, remember always used to compound rapport or influence a client)

Client: "Yeah, my other brother lives in Germany.... But erm.... Ken was always there. I remember getting into trouble at school once and they phoned up and my mum and dad where golfing and.... My brother (Ken) had to come down and they were like, 'You know we need your guardian'. And Ken was like well....You know I must have been fourteen, or fifteen and so he was like twenty four, twenty six—"

Me: "Is this Ken?" (Yes Set Question)

Client: "Yeah... So he said you know I am a guardian..... That's what I mean, he has always been the only one that has not put me down or criticise me...."

Me: "So the only one that has stuck by you". Rhetorical question to convey and compound agreement by leading my client to think, or agree with me verbally. Basically a 'Yes Set Question' to influence, that doesn't really require a verbal answer.

Client: "Yeah."

Me: "Right so you focus your mind on him.... What your other brother (2nd brother) said, and mum said is irrelevant. You have got to understand that their pain has got to go somewhere.

Client: "Mmmmm." Said whilst nodding her head in agreement as my client tends to do.

Me: "And it just happened to be on you. Because you were in that situation at the time. But it was your dad decision not to go to hospital. That was his issue, his choice in life. Nothing to do with you.

Client: "That's it, they.....erm the week erm—"

My client was fumbling for the right words to say so I reinforced the message by saying: "You couldn't have forced him because he was stubborn."

In agreement my client said: "Yeah

Dear student, remember that in order to reinforce a message into a client's subconscious as fact, it is very important to repeat that message until the client fully takes it on board as fact. In this case, the message is to change the association of blame (neurological pain) to an association of realising that she was, and is innocent of any wrong doing that led to her dads death (association of released pain that gives pleasure). This was continued throughout this session due to the importance. The reason being was because this was the main event-cause to her drinking, feelings of guilt, anger and loss with regards to her dad.

Me: "There is nothing you could have done to take him to hospital is there?"

Client: "No."

Me: "Nothing. So why feel guilty about it, because you feel guilty about it because you feel abandoned by him. But that was his decision. You can't change it."

Dear student, the 'conflicting statements' of 'feel guilty' was said twice and that of 'feel abandoned', so once again I had subconsciously reminded my client of her past feelings that she can now reflect on with her growing knowledge from an external view of reality. That knowledge being the new perception of her past. She did positively reflect because her reply was as follows.

Client: "No."
Me: "It was his decision and that is it. He made the wrong choice in life…. And he paid the consequences for it. But why should you also pay the consequences for his decision that he made."
Silently replied, due to being in deep though, my client said: "I shouldn't," then spoken in a normal tone, "Like you say I feel abandoned by him…as well…. And that hurts."
Me: "And there is nothing on earth can change that." I had been referring to his death and not my client's thoughts on abandonment in which I made clear in my next spoken words.
Client: "I know."

Dear student, emotions of guilt and blame brought on by having the wrong perception of being at fault of a person's death, those feelings are totally different from the feeling of abandonment. This must be addressed with my client, and I did as follows.

Me: "He has gone. He made a decision. What you can do is change your perception of it. He abandoned himself. He let himself down. He let everybody down that he knows. His friends and family. It is not just you… it is everybody he let down and he let himself down. That was his decision. His issue. Can't be change. You are completely innocent of anything."
Client: "Mmmmm."

Dear student, please note that my client, in reference to her dads death, had previously said, "I feel abandoned by him". So clearly she had felt isolated in her emotional abandonment. She never once mentioned the fact that her mum and two brothers had also been abandoned. My spoken sentences had made my client aware that she wasn't alone because everyone around her dad had also been abandoned. This gave her a sense of comfort.

Why had she not previously realised that everyone had been abandoned? The answer is simply because previous to the session, she had an internal perception of reality, and as a consequence she couldn't previously see the full picture (external view) of her situation until led to do so by me. Hence why therapy for this client was so important.

I continued: "And that is the situation (Authoritarian). Now if you focus your mind on feeling abandoned all the time... then you will always be ill.... And the fact is.... He did what he did. His decision. Nothing to do with you. His life is separate to yours. Your mum's life is separate to yours. Your brother's lives are separate to yours. They are their own people. You can't change people—"

Client: "That's the thing with my mum and life.... My mum doesn't really have a life so she—"

Me: "Do you have a life?"

Client: "Yeah but she [mum] doesn't like it. At the moment erm... if I am in the house and I am not doing anything, she says, 'What are you doing, what are you sitting there for? Why don't you go out and do something.' So we kind of like butt heads all the time over the stupid of things—"

Me: "Mmmmm." (Mirroring my client's previous tone to secure (compound) rapport).

Client: "And so recently I have been going out more. Not out, out." My client was referring to not going out to bars and clubs drinking. "You know just going out for the day, you know going to see friends. Going for a coffee, staying out for lunch erm... And I have been staying at friend's houses just when it's been stressful because like I say.... We end up.... not arguing because I won't argue back with her [mum] because... I... I'm... to be truthful I am intimidated by her. So I won't argue back. So if it is a stressful situation, I walk away from it rather than make it—"

Me: "Mmmmm."

My client continued her previous sentence: "A stressful situation. I know I will always have to go back home, and we will have to talk it through, or... her shout at me and me say right this is why I did this, and this is why I did that. You know I'm sorry blah, blah, blah....but when it gets like that I find it easier for me to walk away...than to actually face it then."

Me: "Well you have done the right thing. But you living with your mum isn't healthy is it?"

Client: "No," said in agreement and with a confident strong conviction of defiance against her mum.
Me: "It is not healthy for your psychological health."
Client: "No."

Dear student, please note that I did not say, 'mental health' at the end of my last spoken sentence to my client. What my client was doing was walking away from conflict with her mum by going out. That was the right thing to do. Even so by going out for coffee etc she was also running away from her responsibilities. Those being to set a plan of action to overcome her negative living situation, because then she could rebuild her relationships with her children, and as such rebuild her life. This must be addressed within this session when the time is right.

I continued: "Or physical health—"
Client: "No because like I say I just literally can't win [can't win confrontation with mum] because if I am in at home… You know it's not like I sit there with my feet up watching television all day. You know I do washing, I'll hover [vacuum clean]. I'll clean up… you know… I cook my own meals and buy my own food, I do my own washing. So I'm not… at home living with mum like, 'Oh yeah this is the life of Riley [easy life]' I do all that myself… and I, you know, I help out, clean up like I say… do all that. Take the bins out… And she is like, 'Oh you know you are just sitting in all day, you should be out, it's a nice day,' And all of that. So when I have been recently going out… she is then, 'Where are you, what are you doing?' And when I've come back its like, 'What have you been doing?'
In agreement to what my client had verbalised, I said: "There is nothing you can do to please that woman."
In agreement, after I had compounded rapport my client said: "No, no nothing."
Me: "Nothing." (Mirroring)
Client: "Nothing."
Me: "Absolutely nothing. That is her issue—"
Client: "Mmmmm."

Dear student, notice the securing of rapport with the use of agreement, mirroring tone and words used by me.

Me: "She is still projecting her pain of her loss—"
Client: "Mmmmm." Said whilst nodding her head in agreement.
Me: "She has lost her husband…. That pain has got to go somewhere, and so she is still taking it out on you… That is her issue. That is her wrong doing. Nothing to do with you is it?"
Client: "She does it with my children as well."
Me: "You are not going to change her."
Client: "No."
Me: "You can only change yourself."
Client: "Mmmmm." Once again said whilst nodding her head.

Dear student, have you noticed how my client's perception of her situation has changed for the better? And continues to change due to my simple approach in educating her via my leadership, knowledge, experience, and by keeping her relaxed. She is now seeing her situation from an external view of reality instead of her limited internal destructive warped view of reality.

Me: "Right… you said to me that you have life…. Do you think that drinking is having a life?"
Client: "……No not really… I mean some days I do just go out and have a drink, but there are other things that I do. Like I say, go to the cinema, out for lunch, or meeting friends in a bar with their little kids. You know normal things—"
Me: "Mmmmm."
Client: "It's not just a case of going out and drinking. That is when it gets stressful, that's when I do that."
I then verbalised in an authoritarian way, and tone to represent fact when saying: "Which makes you more stressed."
Client: "Yeah."
Me: "So your coping mechanism to stress is wrong."

Dear student, please note that I had not asked her questions to give her the freedom of choice. I had again verbalised as fact in an authoritarian way to lead my client to agree with me. These facts seep deep into her subconscious as fact, without question, for positive change because she is relaxed, with her conscious guard down, and because of the way I had verbalised with use of a commanding tone. Simple, affective and skilful.

As led my client agreed: "Yeah."
Me: "Your coping mechanism to stress is to drink.... Which creates more stress." (Authoritarian again)
Client: "Mmmmm." Said in agreement whilst nodding.
Associating the anchor of drink to the negative I said: "You have lost your job, lost your house—"
Client: "Mmmmm."
I continued: "Your kids basically... your health—"
Client: "Mmmmm."
Compounding the associated negative to the drink anchor, I said: "All because of drink...." After making the negative association to the anchor, I then asked a 'Closed-ended question': "So how is that helping your stress?"
Client: ".... It's not."

Dear student, my clients reply was clearly led due to my previous built negative association to the anchor, and the way I had verbalised the question.

My client continued: "I am in a vicious cycle. That's what I mean I need to get out of that cycle... I feel that I am on one of those wheels, and I need someone to knock me off."
Me: "Yeah I understand that. What are your children's names?"
Client: "Sarah and Paul."
Me: "What age is Sarah?"
Client: "She is fourteen."
Me: "What age is Paul?"
Client: "Twelve.... So I've got another stress that at the moment Sarah is just.... She is at that age and.... All my friends say to me—like I say she has lashed out at my mum... she has lashed out at me.... You know she is always shouting and everything is not fair, everything is this that and the other.... And people say to me that it is my fault for putting

her through all of this. And I say no, she is just normal. But mum says to me, 'Well how do you expect her to be.'

Me: "Sarah has lost her house—"

Client: "Mmmmm yeah." Said silently in agreement of my words, and due to the associated self-contempt of guilt of what she is putting her daughter through.

Me: "She has affectively lost her mum."

Client: "Mmmmm." Said with a look of contempt towards herself.

Me: "Obviously she is going to be angry. And that anger has got to go somewhere. So she lashes out at you and others. And rightful so (justified anger) She is getting to an age where she is now more aware."

Client: "Mmmmm." Said in agreement.

Me: "She is more aware and understanding."

Dear student, my client had previously tried to justify her daughter's anger as being normal due to her age of being a teenager. My client's assumptions and perception of the anger had been wrong. My client's friends were right, that being that her daughter's anger was my clients fault. I had therefore given a reason for Sarah's anger as a justification for lashing out. This had indirectly changed my client's previous thoughts without the need of being direct in telling my client that she was wrong. My approach affects my client on a powerful subconscious level for positive change because I had led her to think differently without the need of creating confrontation. Again simple, affective and skilful.

Client: "But she is also erm… She has been stealing from me. She like comes round when I am not in… She will go through my room….And I mean like the other day I went home and my drawers were literally open… Like she has always borrowed my jumpers, and my tops, and stuff. And she took this once." My client pointed to a bracelet on her wrist and then said, "Erm because I don't usually take it off, and if I do it is on my bedside table. And I didn't notice at first, and I was like where is my bracelet? Had I taken it off….? And I just like phoned her up and said have you taken my bracelet. She said yeah that she had borrowed it. And I said well that is a special bracelet, it's very expensive, it is not something that a fourteen year old should be running around with." Pointing at her trainers my client said, "And she did it when I bought these trainer. You know they are expensive trainers and… they were still in their box…. And I came back from wherever I had been, and she had taken the box. My iPad…. You know she is taking these things but she is not asking me you know. Even just a text like, 'Mum can I borrow your iPad'."

Dear student, why do you think Sarah is taking her mums things without asking for permission? Give it some thought before reading on.

Me: "Because she has lost all respect for you—"
Client: "Yeah, yeah basically yeah."
Me: "And why should she respect you?"
Client: "Mmmmm." Nodding in agreement of me having a good point.
Me: "You have let her down."
Silently spoken due to the associated guilt to the truth in what I had said, my client replied: "I know."
Me: "You have let your son down."
Client: "Mmmmm."
Using my client's emotions brought on by her past feelings of abandonment from her dad, I said: "You are angry at your dad, for abandoning you…" I then associated those same emotions through the eyes of my clients children by saying, "But that is exactly what you have done to your kids—"
Client: "Mmmmm."
I continued on the same associated path when saying: "….You have done exactly the same. You are not dead but you are not there for them—"
Client: "Mmmmm."
Me: "So you have done the same to them. So they are angry the same as you are angry at your dad."

Dear student, I had made my client realise that what she was doing to her kids is what her dad had done to her, that being emotionally affecting them due to abandonment. The upsetting emotion that my client felt of abandonment from her dad was reassociated, within my client's subconscious, as her kid's emotion due to my client's abandonment of them. What a fantastic reassociation of an emotion, which my client had already felt, for the benefit of my client and her children. I had led my client to see, and feel the external view of reality from her children's perspective instead of her limited internal view. My client now knew how her kids felt because she could relate to the emotional abandonment, and as such my client now has a deep emotional understand of why her daughter was venting anger towards her and others.

Affecting a client on an strong emotional level has a very powerful impact on changing their behaviour for the better. Remember that depressed, stressed, warped thinking people, that don't get therapy, cannot make logical connections between their own behaviour towards others, and their past until it is pointed out to them by a skilled therapist. Once this connection is made, as led by a therapist, then the person changes. In this case the change is made because my client, now that she knows, doesn't want to continue to put her kids through what she had gone through with her dad.

This is why I love my job. To have the skills and ability to change a person's life is extremely rewarding. Let us now continue with this client case study.

Client: "Yeah... this is why... I like... before I started drinking again recently... I was—we (her kids) were building up a relationship ... But whenever we were doing something, even if it was just doing something like baking cakes. We were messing about flicking each other with flour, and my mum came in and she was like, 'Oh you should do it this way.' I was like. 'Mum you know... you tell me I need to spend time with my children. I am trying'. But she is always.... coming in...."

Me: "Interfering?"

Client: "Interfering whenever erm... like I say erm... I said to Paul, 'Oh I'll take you for your hair cut.' And mum was like, 'I'll take him!' And I was like, 'No I'll take him.' And then Paul said, 'No, well actually mum... can you just give me the money and I will go after school?' I said yeah no problem. Then my mum was like, 'Well do you really think you should trust him?' I said well he gets off at the bus stop with his friends anyway. He has been going to that hairdressers for years. He knows him. I trust him, the hair dresser so...."

Me: "Mmmmm."

Client: "And he is responsible.... He is a good kid....Erm."

Me: "Is there any way of getting out of your mothers, because it is not healthy you being there."

Client: "That is what I am trying to look at."

Me: "Part of your recovery process.... is getting away from your mother." That had been said in an authoritarian way, and not a question of choice because I knew I was right.

Client: "Mmmmm." Clearly my client was in agreement.

My client had previously agreed that her mum was interfering so I said, "She is interfering..."

Dear student, I had mentioned interfering again as an influential 'Yes Set command' to lead my client to be fully compliant in committing to what needed to be done. That being to leave her mother's house for her own place.

Client: "Mmmmm." Said in agreement.
Me: "I think.... She is probably jealous of you building a relationship with your children, and she doesn't want you to build a relationship."

Dear student, I know that my clients mum had told her to spend more time with her kids. That gave the impression that she, the Grandmother wanted my client, her daughter, to build a good relationship with her own children. Regardless of what she had consciously said, her subconscious behaviour told a different story of sabotaging the relationship between her daughter and Grandchildren. That is a perfect example of 'Cognitive Dissonance'.

'Cognitive Dissonance' describes a person's conflicting contradictory state of mind between their conscious and subconscious mind. 'Cognitive Dissonance' is an unhealthy state of mind in having inconsistent thoughts, attitudes, beliefs, values or behaviours. This subject I have previously covered in an earlier volume book.

Client: "Well my therapist, when I was in counselling first, she erm—because I wasn't drinking my mum use to drive me there and she would wait in the waiting room. And after the second session the councillor said to me, 'Do you think you could get the bus here?' and I said yeah it's no problem. There is a bus stop is outside. She said, 'Well I don't think it is good having your mum here.'...."
Me: "Mmmmm."

Dear student, my client uses 'Mmmmm' a lot to convey agreement with me, and as such so did I throughout the session as it helps in building and compounding rapport, which results in a compliant client for the benefit of positive change. Remember in the previous volume, my stop smoking client said 'yeah' a lot and as such so did I. I am pointing this out to you so that you realise that as a therapist you have to adapt to suit the client's needs.

Client: "Erm... and then one session we were talking, and we talked a lot about the relationship with my mum, and my councillor said, 'You have talked about your relationship with your dad and your relationship with your mum, I think in some ways....your mum was jealous of the relationship you had with your dad—"
Me: "Mmmmm."
Client: "Because there is twelve years difference between me and Ken, and a ten years difference between me and Martin (Her other brother in Germany) so mum was my age when she had me."
Me: "Mmmmm."
Client: "So basically she had just got her life back. You know the kids where off secondary school, and then she got pregnant again with this little girl (the girl being my client). And like I say I was always little daddy's girl. If I wanted something Daddy got it me. You know I was a spoilt girl I admit that, spoilt little girl.... And that is what my therapist said. She said, 'I think... your mum...'"
Me: "Mmmmm."
My client continued her sentence: "She is jealous of the relationship."
Me: "She is.... That is correct."
Client: "And I think... I've said... I've got that into my head the way she interferes when I am with the children. Like I say erm... For example it was both their birthdays last month (my client's children's birthdays) and I organised both parties, and gave them what they wanted, but both of them said don't let Grandma there."
Me: "Mmmmm."
Client: "My mum got upset about that.... And she was like – 'Why don't you want me there?' to me. And I said... 'No!'"
Me: "As if it is your fault?"
Client: "Yeah... so she was like, 'So I have to come and drive you there, but that's it.' I said, 'No you don't have to drive us there. I can find a way of getting myself there, and I can get the other kids mums to get them there so it's not a problem.' And you know I paid for it, and I didn't

ask her for anything. But she was very put out [upset] by that and erm...."

Me: "Mmmmm so you have got to understand that your mum has got issues. She had got very serious issues—"

Client: "Mmmmm."

Me: "She is jealous of the relationship between you and your kids."

Client: "Yeah Mmmmm."

Me: "She does not want you to recover. If she wanted you to recover she wouldn't be putting you down would she?" (No Set Question)

Client: "No!"

Dear student, with regards to my client coming for a session with me to overcome her alcoholism, remember that her mum had previously said to her that she has done everything [to try and recover], so what's the point in trying anything else because you will just fail at that.

My client's self-worth had been damaged by her mum to the point that her mums put downs made my client think 'why should she bother to seek help to recover'.

That for me was enough proof that her mum doesn't want her to recover. She is a toxic person in my client's life. As such, what I had said to my client was justified, that being, "She does not want you to recover. If she wanted you to recover she wouldn't be putting you down would she?" I was right, hence the justification to what I had said.

The relationship between them has been damaged for years, and the point of this session is help my client recover from alcoholism. I cannot change her mum, she is not my client, so it was best focusing on my client's needs. And with regards to her toxic mum, she is best removed out of my client's life for now, and that will greatly help in in the recovery of my client. Time spent on trying to rebuild the relationship between them just adds more stress to my client, and as a consequence would prolong the drinking problem. So it is best to focus on what matters. Those being my client's true needs of removing toxic people from her life, focusing on her recovery, and what makes her happy. For example being around her children and positive people that make her happy.

Always remove toxic people from your life, regardless of who they are. I assure you that life is so positive without them.

Me: "Your other brother doesn't want you to recover because they [mum and Brother Martin] want to project their pain onto somebody else. They want you to suffer because it makes them feel better about their insecurities, and their issues in life. Their jealously, their anger and everything else. You are their projection of that—"

Client: "Mmmmm."

Me: "You are doing them a favour by drinking."

Client: "Mmmmm well that was it. Last night, yesterday I was feeling erm... very anxious and then I was very calm because I knew I was coming here. I was like looking forward to being able to just—because everything you have said, it is like you are looking into me. You can read it all."

Me: "Mmmmm." Said with a smile on my face to convey pleasure in the fact that my client has recognised my abilities as a therapist. She clearly trust and believes in me.

Client: "And I was looking forward to it... until last night when my brother [Martin from Germany] phoned' He was like, 'Why are you bothering with that?' —"

Me: "BOOM! There you go."

Dear student, I had said: "BOOM! There you go" because what my client had just said had justified my previous sentence of: "Your other brother doesn't want you to recover....." The BOOM! Is said to represent the reality brick hitting her in response to her recognition that I was right. As she stated herself when saying, "Because everything you have said, it is like you are looking into me. You can read it all." An amazing thing for a client to say and proof of her trust in my abilities as a therapist, and the strong rapport between her and me.

Client: "And then because, like I say, Ken had made an appointment with my alcohol worker that I have not seen for two years. I did that off my own back... I got in touch with them—"

Dear student, my client had contradicted herself in her last spoken words to me. First she had told me that Ken, her brother had made the appointment with her alcohol worker, and then she had claimed that she had got in touch with the alcohol worker off her own back. I didn't acknowledge this contradiction to avoid confrontation, and embarrassment for my client. Plus the fact that regardless of who had reached out to her alcohol worker for an appointment, it was a positive step forwards for her.

I replied: "Which is fantastic."

Client: "And I have an appointment for tomorrow, and my other brother said, 'Well you have done it before and failed so why try again?'..."

Me: "The one in Germany?" (Yes Set Question).

Client: "Yeah."

Me: "So what is this telling you about your mum and that brother?"

Dear student, my last question to my client was an 'Open Ended Question'. I had asked it to test if my client had been fully listening to me, had she understood and agreed with what I had previously suggested to her. That being that Martin and her mum don't want her to recover.

Client: "Well that is it."

Not the detailed reply that I had wanted so I continued to suggest by saying: "They don't want you to recover. And do you know why they don't want you to recover? Because you are a projection of their pain."

Client: "Yeah Mmmmm."

Me: "They want you to be in pain because it makes them feel better. Yeah and that is what it is all about. So.... you cannot help them. You cannot change them. You need to close off from them. And you need to focus on you. What your mum thinks, what your brother [Martin] thinks is irrelevant—"

Client: "Mmmmm."

Me: "They are just projecting their pain from the loss of their dad and husband.... And they need to blame somebody. They are jealous of your relationships. They don't want you to recover. They don't have your best interest at heart. They don't care. That is the reality of the situation. There is nothing, there is no amount of kindness that you can do to them to change them.

Client: "Mmmmm."

Me: "You have got to walk away. Whether they are family or not, this is about your psychological health that is important, and they are going against everything that you want to achieve."

Client: "Mmmmm."

Dear student, once again take note that I had said 'psychological health' and not 'mental health' in order to avoid a negative fearful association of mental illness. Please notice that I do the same throughout this session. I have pointing this out a number of times so I won't be bringing this to your attention again.

My client looked happy because I had given her a solution to one of her problems. She had agreed with everything I had said, so she was listening and understanding me.

Remember that people with low self-esteem, people that self-harm, have a warped perception of reality. They are not capable, without help, of seeing a logical solution to their problem. And you know why that is. The depression and stress causes a 'Trans-Derivational Search (TDS)'. Their conscious mind has gone on a journey and as a consequence they exist in life in a subconscious trance state which makes them vulnerable to suggestion. The suggestions to my client from her mum and one of her brothers was always negative, so of course that had prolonged my client's issues. Hence why the toxic people must be removed from her life. My client clearly felt relief that I'd justified a reason for her to walk away from the toxic people in her life. She no longer needed to be a victim of their pain. She had no reason to feel any guilt by walking away due to my given logical justification on doing so.

Me: "Right, you have got to walk away. And that is the first stepping stone…. of your recovery. In order to recover you have got to have… a stepping stone of goals."

Client: "Mmmmm."

Me: "And your first goal… is to get away from your mother. Don't even bother talking to your brother in Germany. Don't image that you have got a good relationship with him because you have not, and you never will have."

Client: "Mmmmm."

Me: "You have got to recover your life, and then get in touch with them. And this is what I have done. And if they put you down… because of your recovery… you have not lost anything by not being in touch with them have you?"

Client: "No."

Dear student, notice that I was talking her about her recovery as fact without question. This of course is very positive for her subconscious mind.

Me: "So they are not healthy for you."

Client: "No!"

Me: "Even your own kids want nothing to do…. with your mother."

Client: "Yeah."

Me: "It is causing them grief. It is breaking the relationship up between you and them."

Client: "Mmmmm."

Me: "For you to have a relationship—and your time is running out. Your daughter is fourteen... Right...by the time she gets to sixteen... eighteen she will have her own life."

Client: "Mmmmm."

Me: "She will be going out with her friends more, and you are irrelevant (Negative association to not improving their relationship). You have got to do it now. Take them to Disneyland or wherever (Positive association to improving their relationship). Where do you get money from... for your alcohol?

Client: "Just erm... benefits."

Me: "You get benefits?" (Yes Set Question)

Client: "Yeah ESA [Employment Support Allowance] and erm... I still get the erm child benefit. My ex-partner gets the majority of the child working tax, and the child tax breaks because.... I get the child benefits. But then I pay for things like school trips."

Me: "Mmmmm."

Client: "Like I say when they need new school shoes, and I paid for their parties. So it's not like I am spending it all on you know [alcohol]. I make sure that when they need something... they get it you know."

Me: "Right." Raising my tone to move on to a different topic, "So the problem as I see it is.... Your perception of yourself... is wrong. Your perception of your situation... with your dad... was wrong. Right...his issue, it was his decision. He didn't want to go to hospital. There is nothing you could have done to get him to the hospital. Nothing! Right. Your mother and your brother blame you because they want to project their pain—"

Client: "Mmmmm." Said whilst nodding her head in agreement as she often does when saying, Mmmmm.

Me: "They have no interest in your health...at all. They don't care. They are jealous... right. You have got to get rid of them... whether they are family or not. I did the same with my dad. My dad, I have not seen for over ten years—"

Client: "Mmmmm."

Me: "Because he was negative, he was putting me down all the time. Just because they are blood, just because it is a mum or a dad, if it is not healthy for my psychological health... I walk away."

Client: "Mmmmm."

Me: "I've never been happier. You have got to walk away. You are never going to recover by having that negativity...in your life..... Are you. You have got to walk away. You have got to get away from them. Get your own place... and start rebuilding your life there—"

Client: "Mmmmm."

Dear student, what I had said with regards to my dad is true. I mentioned it so that my client realises that I can relate to her situation. This builds an even stronger rapport between my client and me, and proves to my client that walking away from toxic people is the best option.

Notice that at the beginning of some sentences I had verbalise the word 'right'. I had done the same several times within this session. The word 'right' is a signal to her subconscious that what I had had said, and, or was about to say is right. Again this is very positive for her recover as it leaves no doubt within her mind. This is because the use of the word 'right' allows her subconscious to take on what I say as fact. It eliminates uncertainty so that she can move forwards in life with a clear focused mind without dwelling on other alternatives. In other words my clients mind becomes free from the burden of being lost in a fog of conflicting thoughts.

Me: "Right that is very important. So that therapist, when she said, 'Don't... bring your mother'. She was correct."

Client: "Mmmmm."

Me: "Not healthy. The less time you spend around your mother... the less time you speak to your brother in Germany.... The healthier it is for you. You have never had a positive conversation with your brother in Germany have you?"

Client: "Mmmmm." Said in agreement that she hasn't had a positive conversation with him.

Me: "He has never complimented you. So no wonder you have low self-esteem. If you get a child and constantly put them down.... is that child going to be positive in life?" (No Set Question)

Client: "No."

Me: "No (mirroring). Right. You cannot change them. What you can do is change yourself and your perception of yourself." I continued to talk in an uplifting positive, almost excitable tone, "You are actually a very intelligent person (boost ego). And you are actually very with it. You just lack understand in certain areas... of yourself. So I am going to educate you on all of that, so that you can change you. You can start to recover as of today. You have already.... Two years ago you stopped drinking for eight months. So we know you can do it."

Client: "Yeah."

Me: "It is just extending that for the rest of your life. Drink is not the solution is it?" (No Set Question)

Client: "No."

The following was said by me in a down beat way: "You have got no money, no savings, because you are spending it on drink."

Client: "Mmmmm."

Me: "How are you ever going to get a house of your own, even renting by spending thousands of pounds... on drink—" (Negative association towards the continuation of drinking)

Client: "Mmmmm."

I continued my sentence by saying: "And self-abuse... I mean come on, how much is a bottle of vodka?"

Client: "Six ninety nine (£6.99) for a half bottle...."

Me: "So a full bottle is over twelve pounds. It is really expensive to drink. And then you are just a zombie. You are in bed all day, and you are not eating correctly. Where are the minerals? Where is the protean and vitamins in your body? You don't have any... At what point... is your liver, your body going to say.... Fuckyou! I can't cope with this anymore. It has already sent you signals hasn't it?"

Client: "Yeah."

Me: "And you have ignored it haven't you."

Client: "Mmmmm."

Me: "What signals has it been sending you? You shake don't you?"

Dear student, I had used the expletive word of 'Fuckyou' in order to shock my client. It was an expression of anger from her body to tell her to stop abusing herself. The use of the word emphasises the seriousness of her situation.

Also I had notice that my client's hands had been shaking as soon as she had arrived for therapy, so I had fed that observation back to my client in my last spoken sentence. This adds to the build-up, and continuation of negative associations towards drinking alcohol, which of course leads to a stronger abreaction.

At this point of the session, forty three minutes had passed and my clients tone was subdued. This was perfect because it was a strong indication that the leading of my clients subconscious to feel a negative association towards drink was working.

Client: "Yeah I shake... a lot. I shake... I shake a lot but then... when I am really anxious... I get really shaky.... Like my friend who I have been staying with who erm... he's erm a recovering alcoholic. He has been out, you know where he has had no place to live. So he has been helping me by saying to me, 'Right this is what you need to do.' And he has been letting me stay, like on his settee. And even like this afternoon, and he has done it like a few time. But when he is working, he just says, 'Right go to my flat... just chill out, watch TV'."
Me: "So there are people there for you—"
Client: "Yeah."

Dear student, notice that when my client had been verbalising what she had stated her male friend had said to her, she had used the word 'right' at the beginning of both dialogs. It is possible that her friend had used the word 'right' at the beginning of his sentences, however it is more likely that my client was unknowingly mirroring my use of the word 'right' to convey fact, and the right thing to do. This was due to the strong connection (rapport) between my client and me.

Me: "What is his name?"
With an uplifting tone due to my client's positive associations to this man, she replied: "Darren.... And he has even to the point where you know he has said give me Ken's number. You know if I am really worried about you...I can [phone him]..."
Me: "Right focus your attention on the people that care about you. Darren and Ken care about you. Your kids care about you but they are pissed off. They have had enough. They are young, and they want a life. And they don't have the life that—the family life that they want. You should be taking them to Disneyland. And enjoying their youth. And you are not."
Client: "Mmmmm."
Me: "Right. You don't have a life with them as such... yeah. You are just existing around them—"
Client: "Mmmmm."
Me: "Yes you organised a party and that was living, but it was short lived. It should be everyday living. And you are not living every day. Some days you are just existing."

Client: "Mmmmm yeah that is what I mean... The days when we have tried to do things...like we just sit down making a big bowl of popcorn...."
Me: "And your mum has interfered."

Dear student, finishing off a client's sentence, as I had done in my last sentence, must only be done if you are one hundred percent sure that you are right in its contents. Done right it compounds a very strong connection with the therapist and the client. It reinforces the clients trust and belief in their therapist of having full understanding of their thoughts. The client and therapist become one in a common reality of agreement and mutual understanding. Very powerful, and a must for a successful session.

Client: "Yeah my mum in coming in every five minute," with a raised tone speaking as her mother my client said, "Do you want this, do you want that," now back speaking as herself, "And even they say, 'Grandma will you just leave us alone'."
Me: "She is trying to sabotage. But look what your kids want. Your kids want a relationship with you... because they have told..... you that they don't want their Grandma there." Said in relation to the birthday party, "They wanted you there, to build a relationship with you. So you are in a very, very lucky position.... That you have still got them wanting you (positive association to building on their relationships). You have not lost them yet. But if you carry on then you are going to lose them (negative association if she continues to drink). They are fourteen and twelve... you have got a limited time... with your fourteen year old."
Client: "Mmmmm."
Me: "Right. Once she gets to sixteen and that, she is going to go off with her friends on holiday and stuff like that. So she won't need mum anymore. At the moment she still needs you... so you have a limited time, and I am talking.... now today. From this day forwards."
Client: "Mmmmm."
Me: "You are going to have to get rid of your mum... No benefit to you whatsoever. Years from now... months from now when you have recovered, and you have got your own place and that, then get back in touch with your mum. But for now it is not healthy for you. Don't even bother phoning your brother in Germany. He only slags you off and puts you down anyway."
Client: "Mmmmm."

Me: "What is the point? Don't attract that negativity into your life. Stick with Darren. Stick with Ken. Stick with your children and have a goal. And the goal is to get your own place... right. This is your number one goal to get your own place, and then you can build on that relationship. So that your mother doesn't interfere. Even say to Darren, 'Can I come around your flat and cook with my daughter'." (Always give clients solutions)

Client: "Mmmmm."

Me: "And then you don't have your mother interfering."

Client: "Yeah."

Me: "You know, do that... and he is more than willing to help you. And then she is not there. In fact don't even have your children round your mum's house... Why would you even invite them round? Every time you are with them go out with them. Go out with them... and enjoy life. Go for a walk in the country with them. It doesn't have to cost anything. You know go to the park with them. Walk through a nice woodland or whatever. You don't have to spend a lot of money. But you have got to get them away from your mum. It is simple little things like that... they make a massive positive difference."

Client: "Mmmmm."

Dear student, notice how I had simplified her problem. Remember that depressed clients cannot rationalise logically, so it is important for you as a therapist to simplify their problem, by giving simple achievable solutions to their problem. Set goals where there were none originally.

Had you notice that I had repeated the advice from earlier on leaving her mums and not talking her brother in Germany. Repetition helps for the advance to seep deep within my client's subconscious for positive change. Repetition from the therapist is very important to secure positive change for the client.

Me: "You are an intelligent woman aren't you?" (Ego boost)

Client: "Yeah."

Me: "You have just lost control."

Client: "Yeah well that is it. I have got erm...."

My client hadn't continued her sentence, so I changed the subject because I was ready to move on with the session. I said: "Now when it comes to anxiety. Anxiety is not real. Now if you had a broken arm... that broken arm is real and the cause is real, and so the effect is real. But with anxiety... anxiety is a state of mind. It is a perception. Right. It is not an actual physical thing is it?" (No Set Question)

Client: "No."

Me: "It is your minds perception of something.... That is not real right. So let me ask you a question (command because no choice was given). What is reality?"

Client: ".... What you do what happens... What happens that's real like? When it starts raining that's reality...."

Me: "Erm yeah..."

Client: "Erm....."

Dear student, disregarding the thought of real rain right now, as you know, what a person's perception of what is real may only their perception [imagined version] of reality. This means that what my client thinks is real in general, maybe false as only their false-truth. Or only in agreement within the common reality of a small social group. So what my client thinks is real is not necessarily true. For example her perception of being responsible for her dads death.

The consequences of her wrong perception of being responsible for her dad's death, had brought on negative emotions within her which had led to her self-destructive behaviour. She had wrongly justified the negative blame because she had not taken him to hospital. So for my client that was her truth of reality, and as a consequence she punished herself with drink. However, she never had a real reason to feel guilt, or blame because his death was of his own stubbiness and ego of refusing to go to hospital. As such her emotional, and behavioural response of a false failed responsibility was brought on by her false-truth. Her false-truth was mainly due to the negative abusive conditioning from her toxic mum and brother from Germany. In short her mum, brother from Germany and herself where all in the same false-truth reality of the situation. This of course is only in agreement within the common reality of a small social group. This is why my advice of removing her mum and brother Martin from her life until she recovers is justified. In contrast the overall larger common social perception of reality of the same situation is the truth. That being, she was, and has been innocent all along of any wrong doing.

Dear student, remember that perception is only imagination, and that effects a person's emotions that in turn effects their behaviour. Change the perception of any given situation, and the person's emotions and behaviour follow. Interesting I am sure you will agree.

I continued: "But for you as a person what is reality?"

Client: "Me as a person reality was erm….."

Me: "Is reality what you see, is it what you touch, is it what you taste, is it what you smell, is it the here and now?"

Client: "What happens…. Reality is….."

Me: "Your perception of what happens (false-truth), and my perception of what happens could be two different things…"

Client: "Mmmmm."

Me: "We could both be at a funeral… and I could be happy celebrating that person's life, and really grateful that I've known that person, and I am happy that they're no longer in pain. That's my perception of the situation. Your perception of the same situation could be devastation that you have lost that person…. So we are both in the same situation…. that is real, but my reality of it is different to yours… So reality is not what is real is it? Reality is your perception of what is real and not actually the situation—"

Client: "Mmmmm."

Me: "Because your perception of it… is different to mine. You could be devastated and upset, you have lost a loved one. And I could be really happy, even though I have lost that same loved one…. But I am celebrating the life I have had with them, and I am happy for them that they are no longer in pain. So reality isn't what is real is it?"

Client: "No."

Dear student, what a great way of putting my client and myself in the same situation with use of an analogy, this compounds rapport. The analogy was clearly related to her dad's death without the need of mentioning him. It was also a great way of explaining to my client that different people have different perceptions of reality in the same given situation. People have a choice in a given situation, either they have a negative response, or a positive one to the same scenario. Make your choice that helps you in life and that has got to be positive.

Me: "Reality is your perception of what is real… Let us say that you and I are on a beach…. And I have been to this beach before… and you haven't… and you ask, 'Dave what is that out at sea?'"

Client: "Mmmmm".

Me: "And out at sea there is a little black blob. Right. And I say, 'Amy it's a ship' yeah.

Client: "Yeah"

Me: "I am going to go off on one here, and you are going to be thinking – 'What the hell is he talking about'. It will make sense in a minute. And you say, 'What is that out at sea David?' and I say, 'Well it's a ship Amy'… so you look, and within your subconscious mind you have seen a ship before. (Use of personal name are very important as explained in earlier volumes)

Client: "Mmmmm."

Me: "So within your subconscious mind there is a file…. In your mind that knows what a ship looks like in your imagination. So it pulls out that file, and what do you now see? You see a ship."

Client: "Mmmmm."

Me: "But I lied to you because I have been to this beach before and you haven't. And I say, 'Well actually Amy it is an oil rig….' So your subconscious mind then changes the ship file for an oil rig file, and now what do you see?"

Client: "Oil rig."

Me: "An oil rig… You have just been in three different realities. The first reality you saw a black blob. You didn't know what it was. The second reality you saw a ship because I suggested it. And the third…. The third reality you saw what it really is an oil rig. So what happens….? Your mind fills in the blanks of what you actually can't see because it's still a black bob."

Client: "Mmmmm."

Me: "So your mind fills in the blanks of what you can't see, and you actually think you see a ship, and then an oil rig. So you are in the same situation as me….."

Client: "Mmmmm."

Me: "But we are both seeing something different. Therefore reality cannot be what you see. It is how your mind perceives what you see…. Are you with me?"

My client confidently replied: "Yeah."

Me: "I could give you an onion…"

Client: "Mmmmm."

I continued my sentence: "And I could convince you that it is an apple… You would touch an apple… see and apple, smell an apple…. taste an apple. And you would argue all day long that it was an apple. But it's an onion…. Therefore reality cannot be what you see, touch, taste or smell…. Reality is how your mind perceives it."

Dear student, after educating my client on what reality is, I then continued by relating her new knowledge to her past situations of being stressed.

I continued, "Right! So when you are being stressed over a situation, what are you actually getting stressed over? Are you actually getting stressed over the real situation, or your minds perception of it? Do you understand me?"
Client: "Yeah."
Me: "Interesting that...."
Client: "Mmmmm."
Me: "So... your perception of the situation, your perception of your dads situation.... was wrong.... Because it had nothing to do with you... Right... why should you feel guilty... about something that he did....? So your perception of the situation had (past tense) to have been wrong.... You have been punishing yourself all of these years for something that has nothing to do with you.... Just because your brother blamed you, and your mother blamed you.... Because they had to project their pain somewhere. So your perception.....was not real....! It was only your perception of your version of reality... are you with me? In your mind...."
Client: "Mmmmm."
Me: "Why should you blame yourself for something that someone else has done? Your dad did it not you.... So why would you blame yourself for what he has done.....? You not taking him to hospital had nothing to do with you. You was blaming yourself for a decision that he made in life. He wouldn't go to hospital.... That is his fault.... So your perception of blaming yourself... what you saw as reality is not reality at all is it?"
Client: "No."

Dear student, if I do say so myself, wasn't that a fantastic way of changing my clients negative perception of the situation, to one that removed all the responsibility and burden of blame from her. Remember that her original negative perception of the situation, was the event-cause that had led to her self-abuse. Now that her perception of the same event-cause had changed for her benefit, she no longer has a reason to punish herself with drink.

Me: "It was just your imagined thought."
With a pleased look on her face she said: "Yeah." The burden of blame and guilt had been removed.
Me: "So when you get anxious and anxiety... what are you actually getting anxious and guilty over...? Your minds perception of the situation which was wrong..... Does that make sense?"
Client: "Yeah totally."
Me: "Am I right?" (Yes Set Question)
Client: "Yeah."
Me: "Yes. You are intelligent enough to understand it (ego boost)... His decision in life.... Your mother was wrong... to project her pain onto you.... Your brother was wrong to project his pain onto you. Pity them.... Feel sorry for them.... That they are in pain, and they have to blame somebody else's instead of the true person to blame which was your dad."
Client: "Mmmmm."
Me: "It was his decision in life." As an analogy I then said, "If someone decides to go and throw themselves off a cliff... that is their decision..."
Client: "Mmmmm."
Me: "I can't stop them because that is what they want to do. I am not going to blame myself for a decision that they made in life... So your perception of the situation was wrong. Am I right?"
Client: "Yeah!"
Me: "Yeah you accept that?" (Yes Set Leading Question)
Client: "Yeah."
Me: "So what were you punishing yourself for.....? Now yes it is a separate issue feeling abandoned, let's forget that for now. Feeling abandoned is a separate issue... yeah." Saying that gave my client the false impression that I was not going to educate, or continue to mention her feelings of abandonment. By doing so I had kept her guard down so that I had a greater impact within her subconscious mind when saying the following, "Again that was his decision.... He decided not to go to

hospital. He knew he was ill. He knew he couldn't walk so he clearly had a serious illness.... He.... decided not to go. He abandoned his own life. He had enough. He gave up on life... He no longer wanted to live... If he wanted to live he would have gone to hospital wouldn't he?"

My client in a positive understanding agreeable tone replied: "Yeah."

Me: "He gave up. He let everybody down. Not just you... he let himself down. The first person he let down was himself.... The next people he let down was his family.... And the third set of people he let down was his friends.... Right... tough that was his decision. He abandoned himself..... He had given up on life.... That is his issue. Why is that your issue? Is that your issue?"

Client: "No!"

Dear student, I had disassociated my client from feelings of isolated abandonment by once again making it known to her that many people were let down by her dad. I had also compounded the responsibility and blame onto her dad to secure change in my clients perception of the situation, which changes her emotions and behaviour for the better. Again repetition is very important.

I continued: "You have the aftermath of....a decision that he made... You have that aftermath that you need to cope with... You cope with it by understanding it. Your perception of it wasn't reality [alternatively a positive common reality or healthy reality]. It was only your perception of reality in blaming yourself... but why.....? Why would you do that to yourself when it has nothing to do with you?"

Dear student, my last sentence that I had said to my client had been in two stages. Firstly I had asked, 'Why would you do that to yourself'. By asking that question, my client was led to question her own beliefs, and by doing so I had caused a 'Trans-Derivational Search (TDS)' within my client's conscious mind. As a result the second stage of the sentence lead my client with the subconscious influential commanded fact of, 'when it has nothing to do with you'. This influential way of changing my client's perception of a given situation is very powerful and long lasting when reinforced throughout the session. She now realised that her past negative way of thinking about herself was in fact wrong. This gave her back a positive sense of self-control when originally she had been controlled by her negative guilt of blame.

Client: "Because like you say it was (past tense) the way I saw it."
Me: "And you was wrong."
Client: "Mmmmm." Said whilst nodding in agreement. Clearly my client's led change of perception had eliminated her past self-destructive perception of the same situation.
Me: "It's like me and you on a beach... You have seen a ship just because I told you it was a ship, just like your brother told you it was your fault... I've told you it's a ship...well I was wrong because it's an oil rig. There is a different perception. So what you see as reality is how your mind perceived a given situation. Is that onion an apple....?" (No Set Question)
Client: "No."
Me: "No but I could genuinely hypnosis you and convince you that it is an apple... and you would tell me that it is an apple. That would be your reality. From a perception in your mind, and not what is real. So reality is not what is real. Reality is what you imagine it to be as your truth even if it is a false-truth."
Client: "Mmmmm."

Dear student, I had previously explained, to my client, that people can have different perceptions of reality even though they are in the same given situation. I had done that with the use of the beach analogy of looking out to sea and viewing the same object, but seeing it differently. I.e. a black blob, or a ship, or an oil rig. In my last spoken dialog to my client I had reminded her of the analogy because she had understood it. I then related that knowledge to the same situation of her brother telling her it was her fault with regards to their dad's death. This way my client realises that there is a different perception of reality from what her brother's negative perception is of blame towards her. I then reinforced this knowledge by reminding her that I was wrong about the ship because it was an oil rig. This is the same as her brother being wrong with his perception, so there is an alternative. I then reinforced once again that there are different perceptions of reality with the use of the onion analogy. This is use of repetition in order to secure permanent positive change from a negative perception within my client subconscious. This I continued to do throughout the session, and this is why repetition is of such importance. So as a person, if you don't like repetition, then I will remind you once again that being a therapist isn't for you.

I continued the session by first holding up a real pen. Then I said: "We can both look at this... We are not looking at the same pen... Your perception of that pen....cannot be the same colour as my perception. We don't occupy the same mind. You are looking at it from a different angle to me. You are seeing it as a different size to me. We are not looking at the same pen.... So our perception of this pen...is different because we are looking at it from a different angle. Your perception of that colour is different to mine. We are not looking at the same colour. No two human beings occupy the same mind.... Therefore we can't be in the same reality can we?" (No Set Question due to no choice of an answer given)

Client: "No."

Me: "We can be in a common reality....in agreement.... But we can't be in the same reality because we don't occupy the same mind. And reality is a perception of each individuals mind... Are you with me?"

Client: "Mmmmm."

Me: "Now let's say.... We have got two parts of the mind. We have got the conscious mind. The conscious will. You make a conscious decision...."

Client: "Mmmmm."

Me: "And then we have got the subconscious mind.... the imagination. Which.... part of the mind.... on a day to day basis is in control?"

Client: "The subconscious."

Dear student, clearly my client knew the correct answer as being the subconscious because I had previously been educating her. Also notice my use of rapport building and compounding words i.e. 'we', 'our' and 'us' throughout this session where appropriate.

Me: "Yes. Let us say we make a conscious decision – 'I want to go swimming today'..... Subconsciously in the imagination.... we think..." I then made a sound of brrrrrrrgh! to represent the feeling of touching cold water, and then I said, "I bet that water is cold.... How do we know? Because we are not there. Brrrrrrgh! I bet there are a load of kids there from school. I bet it's noisy. Oh I bet it starts to rain. I call this a disaster movie within the mind. You play a disaster movie in your subconscious mind... and what happens? It becomes your reality... You are then convinced... that the water is cold even though you are not there. You are convinced that it is going to be full of kids, and it's not is it. So what happens? What you consciously wanted to achieve.... going swimming, you don't do because your subconscious mind is so powerful—"

Client: "It takes over."

Me: "It overpowers... your conscious will. So which part of the mind is in control? The subconscious. The fact is there are no kids at the pool. The fact is...the water is warm. And if you had gone you would have enjoyed it."

Client: "Mmmmm."

Me: "So what stopped you from going? Your imagination that you perceive as reality...so it stopped you from doing what you consciously wanted to do. Yeah?"

Client: "Mmmmm." Said with nod and a look of interest to what I had said.

Me: "Because your perception of reality is wrong [wrong because it had caused the self-harming]. So let's change this situation to alcohol... Right... You don't want to drink alcohol. Now if you consciously tell yourself – 'I don't want that'. You have subconsciously played a different movie. I am talking to your conscious now, and under no circumstances do I want you thinking about a black cat...." I started to stroke an imaginary cat on my lap before saying, "I am not stroking a black cat.... What are you now imagining?"

Client: "A black cat." She said as she laughed because I was right and she couldn't stop herself from thinking about a black cat. Just the same as you are right now.

Me: "A black cat. The exact opposite of what you wanted to achieve.... So if you say, 'I don't want that alcohol.' Then subconsciously you have already drank it. You can already taste it. You have already deluded yourself that this is going to help you to overcome your problem.... How has alcohol helped you to overcome your problem.....? How has it helped you to overcome anxiety...? What has it brought to your life....? You have lost everything!"

Client: "Everything!" said at the same time as me when ending my last sentence. Which is an indication of strong rapport.

Me: ".... Your home, your boyfriend, your kids, your job, your money, your driving licence...all gone because of alcohol.... Because your perception of reality... of your situation.... is wrong. Reality is not real... reality is a person's perception of a situation. Do you understand that?"

Client: "Yeah," said with a sombre tone as the realisation of the truth of her past perception, and the damage it had done to her life was now consciously known to her.

Me: "You can have one hundred people on the London underground... they are all on the same train. And all one hundred people are in a different perception of reality... They are not actually on that London underground in each individual's perception of reality. One is thinking of themselves on holiday, so much so that they get the emotions of themselves on holiday. And that is what they are seeing. They forget the fact that they are physically on the London underground. That they are on the tube. If you are watching television.... you no longer are sat in the room that you are in are you. You are in that movie—"

Client: "Mmmmm."

Me: "You no longer see the edges of the television. You have actually hypnotised yourself. You are in that movie, so your perception of reality has changed... You are physically still in the same room, but within your mind your perception of reality is that you are in space, or a western, or whatever the movie is about."

Client: "Yeah."

Me: "And at the time of being in it, you can't actually say that you are in it. It is only when you come out of the trance that you think – 'bloody hell I had gone then'..."

Client: "Mmmmm."

Me: "I was there, and then boom you are back in the room. And then you are back into that reality..... So reality cannot be what you see can it? It can't be what you see, touch, taste or smell, it is how you perceive a situation. Your perception of yourself for all of these years.... had been wrong.... Does that make sense?"

Client: "Yes... totally."

Me: "Do you agree with me?" (Yes Set Question)

Client: "Yeah."

Me: "Is that interesting?" (The 'Yes Set Question' was asked because I could see how interested she was.)

Client: "Yeah"

Me: "So what is reality? It is a person's perception of a given situation, and not what you think is real... Because your situation that you thought was real...is not real... You have nothing to blame yourself for... It was real for you at the time, but when you think about it, take a step back and reflect on it...which you have never done because you have always reacted instead of reflect. Reflect and think – 'Actually how is it my fault…. His decision not to go to the hospital…. How is it my fault….? His decision to give up on life…. How is it my fault…? It can't be… nothing to do with me….' So how is it your fault…..?

Client: "It can't be."

Me: "So what are you blaming yourself for?"

Client: "Because my perception was wrong."

Me: "Yes. You were blaming yourself for someone else's decision…. It was his decision… how can that be your—He is in a different reality to you. You can't be in the same reality because you don't occupy the same mind…. Your perception of reality was different to his."

Client: "Yeah."

Me: "His decision… it is tough. Life is tough… tough that he made that decision… get on with it."

Client: "Mmmmm."

Me: "His decision."

Client: "His perceptive was that if he goes [to hospital] he is going to look weak."

Me: "Yeah."

Client: "My perceptive was that if he goes he is going to get help."

Me: "Yes…. So you blamed yourself because he didn't get that help…"

Client: "Yeah."

Me: "But that was his decision…. Men, his ego kicked in."

Client: "Mmmmm."

Me: "What happened, his ego kicked in and he didn't want to look weak…"

Dear student, I had fed back to my client what she had previously said about being weak. I had done that to compound rapport in agreement for continued conformity from my client. My client's replies to my questions were fantastic because they were proof that her perception of the main event-cause to her problems had changed, as led by me.

Client: "Mmmmm."

Me: "He didn't want to go to hospital... 'I'm a Mr tough guy, I can handle this....' Well no he couldn't because it killed him."

Client: "Mmmmm."

Me: "Yeah. You have lost your farther, it is upsetting, but that is now the past. You have got to focus your mind on your children.... And your psychological and physical health .... You have always been focusing on the past, and reacting to it on what your mother said... and what your brother had said, and the fact you didn't take your father to hospital. There is nothing you could do to change that situation... Those were their decisions in life. Right. So your perception was wrong wasn't it?"

Client: "Yeah."

Me: "So let us focus on the here and now.... Of what you need to do... That drink—this is an honest true story this – Last year... a good friend of mine finished with his fiancé. She was an alcoholic. He would find Vodka bottles, Whiskey bottles hidden around the house. And she would drink a little bit of wine with him... but she would get overly drunk with the amount of drink that she had consumed. And he couldn't understand for years why she was so drunk off so little alcohol. What she was doing, she was going to the toilet and drinking Whiskey and Vodka and that, and hiding it. And then she would go back down stairs and continue with a glass of wine with him. So he would think that she was just having a glass of wine which got her overly drunk. And she got worse and worse, and worse. And then he found all the drink bottles hidden around the house.... And erm he ended their relationship. She lost her driving licence. She was found drunk in a supermarket carpark with their baby in the back of the car whilst trying to drive. But she was that drunk she lost her driving licence, and she lost her child. The child went to the father. So she lost her house, her job... she lost her children... she lost erm... her job everything gone right. She became more and more ill. And she started to get skin lesions on her face. She was an alcoholic so she started to get these lesions because her body was giving up... And in the end she committed suicide with alcohol... basically... and she died. And previous to her death, I had said to him, and I said to the family that she would be dead... within twelve months... I said I guarantee she will be dead within twelve months... Her parents... were putting her down... Very similar situation to you. Her parents were putting her down all the time... and they would say to her, 'Oh just get a drink down you'. They were taking her out for lunch and saying, 'Just get a drink down you'. They didn't care... So I said, 'Look she will be dead within twelve months I guarantee she will be dead.' Within six months she was dead. Right. So her perception of reality... was wrong.... Her whole life fell apart around her. Your life is falling apart around you (all negative association to the anchor of drinking alcohol). Now the thing about you is, you are in a very lucky position that you have got Darren and you have got Ken (positive associations to how lucky she is for positive change)."

Client: "Mmmmm."

In an uplifting tone I said: "You are in a very lucky position...that you have still got your kids that want to spend time with you. Her kids didn't."

Client: "Mmmmm."

Me: ".... No body helped her. Not one single person helped her. I couldn't help her because she never came to me for help. I saw the situation. I knew that she needed help, but you can't help people that don't want help... She was so gone in the head. You have not gone in the head... you're still understanding me."

Dear student, the story that I had shared with this client about my friend's alcoholic dead ex-fiancé is true. As I write this I now remember that she posting on Facebook a ranting paranoid status, it was about people that she perceived as sad, people who were passing information on about her to her ex. She was paranoid that someone was telling her ex what she was up to in life from information from her Facebook post. Any logical thinking person would have simply stopped making Facebook post if they didn't want the information to be public. However she was not in a logical place in her head. In fact she was incapable of thinking logically. It was soon after the post that she deleted me from her Facebook friends list because she wrongly thought that I was the one gossiping. The fact is I had not said anything to anyone about her Facebook post. I messaged her to tell her that it wasn't me passing her post on, and her reply was that she sent me a new friend's request. I ignored it because I didn't want to get involved in the negativity between her and my friend. Months later she was dead. Maybe I should have reached out to help her, but it is clear that it would have fallen on deaf ears and been rejected.

I continued talking to my client: "You can set a goal of what you need to do. You need to get away from your mother. You need to stop contacting your brother in Germany. He is only going to slag you off anyway. Why have any contact with him?" without giving my client time to reply verbally, in order to allow her to self-talk within her subconscious, I continued, "Yes it is upsetting. You lose a brother, you lose a mother. But what have you actually lost? Your health... Your psychological and physical health improves. I lost my father and he is still alive."

Client: "Mmmmm."

Me: "I have lost him because he was so negative slagging me off. And putting me down because nothing I ever did was good enough... You know... boom (the reality brick boom). And as an adult I have got to say what is best for me. And what is best for you....?"

Client: "To get away from them."

Me: "You have got to get away... There is no point even communication with your mother because it turns into an argument...."

Client: "Mmmmm."

Me: "Right. She is going to win every time because it is her house...."

Client: "Mmmmm."

Dear student, remember that my client, earlier in this session, had told me that she couldn't win with her mum. So I had simply fed that information back in agreement with her by having said, "She is going to win every time...." I then gave her a reason why by having said, "Because it is her house—" My client had agreed, and this gave my client a good reason, and motivation to move out of her mum's home as part of her recovery.

Me: "Your mum's perception of reality is different to yours. When you learn in life that everybody's perception of reality is different, and there is nothing that is real—We can look at the rain coming down.... I can perceive that as a positive thing and enjoy the smell and that. And another person could perceive the same situation as a negative thing – 'Oh I'm going to get wet, it's cold.' I see it as nature. It is going to bring life. It is something to enjoy. So even though we are both looking at rain... our perception of it... is different. So what we perceive as real... is different due to our different perception even though we are both in the same situation. So your mother is not in a common reality with you is she?" (No Set Question)

Client: "No!"

Me: "She never will be.... She is putting you down projecting her pain. She is jealous of the relationship... between you and your children. She doesn't want you to recover. She doesn't give a shit..."

Client: "Mmmmm."

Me: "Now that is harsh.... But that is the true situation.... Isn't it?"

In agreement my client replied with a nob when saying: "Mmmmm."

Me: "Look at the situation as it is. What is real and what is not. You don't have a good relationship with your mother... You don't have a good relationship with your other brother... you never will.... Because they are not interested.... Yeah. The fact that your mother is even letting you live with her... is for one reason, and one reason only...."

Client: "Because she is in control."

Me: "One is control.... And two it gives her a connection to your children."

Client: "Mmmmm."

Me: "She is not doing it for you... is she? She is not doing it to do you a favour... She is doing herself a favour... because it makes her feel good by putting you down.... That is her issue. Right. Now low self-esteem and all of that is just a state of mind.... It is not real. Now if we sit here, and we go... 'Oh god doom and gloom', and think negative thoughts, the chemical balance of the brain changes.... And it creates endorphins that are unhealthy, so we feel unhealthy" Then I raised my voice to a positive uplifting tone and said, "Now if we sit here now, and put your head up, and do that now... go – 'Whoop I am really excited.' Just do that now, sit differently. Sit like that now with your back straight and go – 'Wahoo I am excited'.

In an excitable tone that mirrored my tone, my client enthusiastically said: "Wahoo."

Upping my voice again to an even more excitable tone I said: "It's brilliant."

Client: "Mmmmm." Said with a huge smile on her face.

Taking as my client I said: "I have got life. I have got to rebuild my family. I have got to rebuild that dynamic of the family. In the end I am going to save up and I am going to be able to take them to Disneyland...." I continued by talking as myself when saying, "Or wherever you want to go. So if you just do that now and think of something positive... and go – 'Wahoo I am excited about that'. Just do that now. Don't ever feel foolish about something. Just go – 'Wahoo I feel excited about it'.

After a brief pause my client once again said excitedly: "Wahoo!"

Me: "I use to tell myself that I had won the lottery. It doesn't matter what it is—"

Excitedly my client said: "Yeah, yeah I have just won a scratch card."

Me: "Yeah... well I kept doing this. And you won't believe by looking at me now but I had a mental break down. My life fell apart. I was losing my house, my health deteriorated, I had a prolapse. A guy of my age having a prolapse is unheard of, but I had severe food poisoning. Prolapses is when your internal wall of your anus comes out due to.... severe food poisoning, and my body broke down. I had a mental break down. I became bankrupt.... I was losing my house. I lost everything. And I thought - 'Fuck this, I ether rebuild my life, or I die'. And that is the choice you have got. You are dying. Do you realise this?"

In a subdued tone of realisation of the fact, my client's reply was: "Mmmmm"

Me: "You are actually dying. You are shaking. Your body is sending you signals that you can't cope, and you are ignoring those signals. You are going down the same root as my friend.... She is dead.....! You know that is the choice in life....live.... or die. And you have got to take a step back and think fu—" I didn't finish the words off, those being 'Fuck this' because I wanted to influence my client to self-talk within her mind for the greater benefit towards change. I then continued, "And I would look in a mirror and go – 'Wahoo I have won the lottery, I have won a prize. I am positive.' And I can remember driving down the road one day... and I would talk positive to myself, because it is very important because very few people will. Darren and Ken will.... No one else will because they don't care."

Client: "You are right."

Me: "So talk positive. It is call affirmations. Positive affirmations. 'I am brilliant me', I use to tell myself I was Jesus Christ. 'I am Jesus Christ'. And if I was walking down the street and I heard someone say – 'Oh God Jesus Christ' I use to go over to them and say, 'Yes my child'. Just so amuse myself. Do silly little things to amuse yourself.... I would look in a mirror and pull faces...." Sticking my tongue out and pulling a face I blurted out, "Blaaaaaaaaaa. Just to amuse myself. If a negative thought comes into your mind, just think, fuck this and think of something positive. I am at Disneyland."

Client: "Mmmmm."

Me: "And that becomes your reality. Because your reality is your minds perception which effects your emotions. So if you close your eyes now and imagine yourself—would you like to be on a roller-coaster?"

Client: "No!"
Me: "Where would you like to be?"
Client: "Erm…."
Me: "On a nice beach?"
Client: "Yeah."

Dear student, remember that my client was in a light trance state, a suggestable state, and as such the following was very powerful.

The following I said in a hypnotic monotone: "Just close your eyes now, and imagine yourself on that beach. Just imagine yourself on that beach. Imagine the waves. Imagine the hot sun. And imagine your children are with you on that beach… Right. Imagine enjoying life. See their laughter. They are spending time with their mum with whom they do love, because they want to spend time with you. Those waves are crashing onto the beach. That lovely sound of those waves. That nice heat on your face from the sun. And now realise how that has changed your perception of reality, and therefore your emotions. How does it emotionally effect you that image? How does it make you feel?"

In a relaxed tone my client replied: "Happy contented."

Me: "Now this is what you can do. That becomes your reality. Your imagination effects your emotions… and your emotions effect your behaviour. It is very important that you remember that…. Imagination, emotions…. behaviour. You change your imagination… your emotions change, and therefore your behaviour changes. So anything that you find that creates anxiety… it's not real is it?"

My client replied with a prolonged: "Nooooo."

Me: "No body is doing anything to you."

Client: "So it is my subconscious."

Me: "Yeah… it is your perception. Your mother is putting you down… so your perception was to feel vulnerable and intimidated. Now me in that same situation would feel sorry for her. She is projecting…. her issues onto you."

Client: "Yeah."

Dear student, notice that I had given my client two different perceptions of the same given situation of being put down by her mum. One negative and one positive from my clients view point. That was important to do now that she has an understanding of there being alternative, or a number of different perceptions from a given situation.

And those perceptions are an individual's choice that effect their emotions and behaviour.

I continued: "So let us say that I am you... and your mum is putting me down and interfering and that. I just look at her and say, 'I genuinely feel sorry for you. I feel sorry that you have never been able to get over the pain of the loss of your husband. And that you are blaming your own daughter.... for your loss.' It was his decision! She has never been able to cope with that loss, so she has got to blame somebody. She has got to project her pain.... Pity that woman!"

Client: "I have just thought of something. It just made me think of that—I am probably going to think of now when she puts me down... like you said pity it. Have you ever seen the Harry Potter films?"

Me: "Yeah."

With a wave of an imaginary wizard's wand my client said: "You know where the 'Boggart' comes out and they go 'Riddikulus' and make it into something funny. That is how—because I love Harry Potter, that is how I will imagine it."

In an excitable tone I boosted my client's ego by saying: "This is how intelligent you are.... Therapy works, and the more childlike you make it, the more ridiculous you make it, then the more success you with have."

Client: "Mmmmm."

Me: "Now you know that... and I hadn't told you right."

Client: "Mmmmm."

Me: "What you do, you change your perception.... If you are in a situation where your mother is putting you down, then imagine her as a goblin.... Change her voice. So if she is saying, or your brother is saying, 'Well don't do that, why would you do that'. For your brother to tell you, 'Why would you come here today' is ridiculous. Does he care about you?"

With a defiant tone to her brother Martin, my client replied: "No!"

Me: "He doesn't give a shit! Doesn't give a shit! So change that voice. He is a goblin," Then in a goblins tone of voice I said, "Why would you do that?" Then back to my own voice, "You know, change it to a ridiculous voice and go – 'Expelliartis, or whatever it is that they say [in Harry Potter]."

My client excitedly corrected me, due to her positive association to anything that is Harry Potter, and said: "Expelliarmus!"

Dear student, my client's positive, happy and enthusiastic association to Harry Potter is now her good feel anchor. This positive anchor was created by my client due to her intelligence of understanding of my explanation of what is needed for self-control of her own emotions, and behaviour in a positive way.

The use of a good feeling anchor, in what was once perceived as a negative situation, changes the perception of the situation to a positive emotional and behavioural controllable one.

I enthusiastically mirrored her tone when saying: "Expelliarmus!" My client body language uplifted, and she had a huge smile on her face. I continued, "Now look, notice your emotion…. Boom. Your emotions changed. Because your imagination changed… towards the situation… Your emotions changed, and then what happened? Your behaviour changed. Because your previous anxiety was not real…"

Client: "Mmmmm."

Me: "Aids and HIV is real—"

Client: "Yeah."

Me: "Cancer is real. A broken arm is real… Low self-esteem… anxiety, depression is not real. They are your wrong perception of yourself, and your wrong perception of your reality of a situation….. Is that fascinating?"

In a positive uplifting tone, as the burden from her past was lifted she said: "Yeah it's brilliant! You know me well."

Me: "So you have been (past tense) wrong… all of these years."

Client: "Yeah."

Me: "You have been wrong all of these years. Your realty of your situation was (past tense) wrong…." I then gave my client a sense of control over her own life, "You are the one in charge… You are the one in charge… You are the one that decides who you want in your life… You are the one that decides. You can start saving those benefits up, instead of spending it on alcohol. You can start saving up were you get to a point where you can get a council house…."

Client: "Mmmmm."

Giving my client a realistic goal I said: "Or get another house and rent…. That is going to happen. It is going to take time, but it is going to happen by saving up that money. So you have got a choice, either abuse yourself with that money, and you are dying (association of pain). Do not delude yourself by thinking any other way. Your body is shaking. Since you have been in this room your body has shook… I can see that you have got alcoholic poisoning… I can tell that your liver... is struggling to cope. And once your liver has gone…. that is it! You are dead…..! Yeah… So your body is sending you a signal… You either listen to that signal and do something about it, or you ignore that signal. By ignoring it….. You are dead!"

Client: "Mmmmm."

Me: "Simple as that…. Think of things you could have done. You could have taken your children to Disneyland. Do they want to go to Disneyland?"

Client: "No. they have never mentioned it."

Me: "They have never mentioned it (mirroring to compound rapport). Where do they want to go?"

Client: "Well they do want to go to America. But they have never specifically said Disneyland."

Me: "Right, so they want to go to America." (Yes Set)

Client: "Yeah."

Me: "Can you afford to take them to America?"

Client: "No."

Me: "Yes you can… How much per year are you spending on drink?"

Client: "….. I wouldn't have a clue."

Me: "I can tell you now, it is thousands."

Client: "Mmmmm."

Me: "Thousands of pounds…. On drink which will alternatively get you to America in twelve months."

Client: "Mmmmm."

Me: "So you can afford to take them to America. Your perception of reality was wrong, and you was putting that money somewhere else that it shouldn't go."

Client: "Mmmmm."

Me: "Stop buying shit!" (The words 'Buying shit' provoked a negative emotional association to anchor's that I wanted my client to reject from buying)

Client: "Mmmmm."

I then compounded a possible anchor item to the associated words 'Buying shit' by saying: "Stop buying (led self-talk - shit) chocolate bars, stop buying (led self-talk - shit)—"

Client: "I never eat chocolate."

Me: "Whatever it is. Alcohol you don't need. There are other things that you don't need that you are buying, and you can save that money up, and you can go to America. Or you can get your own flat... and have your children there with you."

Client: "I can do that."

Dear student, what a great positive led reply from my client. Led because I had made her realise that her goals are simple without spending on drink and other junk. That led reply being 'I can do that'. Her mindset had changed. She now had a goal that was realistically achievable, and more importantly she was rightly led to believe it.

Me: "That's reality. That is an achievable goal... You have got to close off from your parent. From your mother and that brother. Focus on Darren. Ask Darren, 'Do you mind if I come round and cook with my daughter?'"

Client: "Mmmmm well I did say that I was like going to come up this afternoon to go and see him—"

Me: "Yeah."

Client: "After I have been here.... Because that is what I mean, he is interested. He was interested in like this morning. You know [he said] 'As soon as you get back, come to see me at work. I want to know all about it.'"

Me: "Yeah because he is a person who genuinely cares. How long have you known him?"

Client: "Well erm.... It's funny actually because he was a parent in school where I taught, and he went through a divorce.... Erm I could see that he was struggling, and I always said, 'You know, if you ever want to talk...' We just got talking that way. And then when I stopped working I didn't see him, and then I use to see him about.... And then I kept bumping into him in town and he said, 'I thought you didn't live around here'. So I told him it's a long story, and he said that I should go into his works and talk about it. So I said, 'Where do you work?'. And he said this erm café cake shop. So I just went in.... and he came out from the back, and he said he would be done within five minutes. So he said leave my number... And it just went from there. I just got chatting and he said right.... He said if I ever needed to chat... Erm we went out one night just for one drink because he knew about my drinking. And then.... went back—"

Me: "Have an orange juice."

Client: "Yeah well that's it.... We went out and went back to his flat, and he just said, 'You know, you seem so much more relaxed here....' And I said, well I am."

Me: "You are anxious at home because you don't know when your mum is going to snap."

Client: "Yeah and it feels like my safety environment. That's what I call it."

Me: "What age is he?"

Client: "He is older than me. He is nearly Ken's age."

Me: "Are you attracted to him?"

Client: "Yeah... yeah but we are both, you know we are both in that place...."

Me: "Yeah but at some point......"

Client: "Maybe but... at the moment he is you know... a very, very good friend, and he understands me, and listens. Like I say I can go there... and I can be like—And then he says, 'You know right.... There is the TV remote, put whatever crap you want on'. And then an hour later I go, 'Why are you staring at me?' and it's because I'd just gone relaxed...."

Me: "Do you know why? It is because the TV changed your perception of reality.... It is self-hypnosis. You are actually, unknowingly hypnotising yourself, and entering a different World which changed your mindset. So remember this. What I want you to remember from today is.... any anxiety, and that is not real, it is just a state of mind. So you can sit there and imagine yourself on a beach with my children enjoying life. And tell yourself I'm fantastic me.... I am rebuilding my life.... I am getting better... I am coping (positive affirmations). Talk positively to yourself yeah.... Changing your imagination changes your emotions which changes your behaviour. That is the number one thing that I want you... to remember. The next is... the goal of getting away from your mother, and don't even bother contacting your brother in Germany—"

Client: "Well I never phone him, he phones me."

Me: "He phones you when he wants to boost his own ego... when he wants to feel better about himself by putting you down."

Client: "Mmmmm."

Me: "That is what he is phoning you for.... You just don't need that in your life right now... When you have recovered then contact them... And if they still put you down when you have rebuilt your life… then fuck them."

As I said 'fuck them', my client at the same time said: "Fuck them off!"

Me: "It is as simple as that. You have got to be harsh, but that is the reality…. So I think the main thing today—I am not going to use hypnosis today… Today has been about educating. I have touched on many things but the main thing is your perception of reality… and you accept now that you were wrong…. That is a major step forward isn't it?"

Client: "Mmmmm."

Me: "A major step forward, because it changes your perception of the situation. And you start to see from a third parties point of view. People look at reality in different ways. People view reality either internally… or externally or both. I am capable of both… so I can view your internal perception of reality, and I can view my external view of reality of the same given situation. And then I can educate you on that… Okay. For years you have had an internal point of view of reality… It has been very internal, and you have allowed other people to affect you. You have never actually externally… viewed reality to think – 'What is this situation. Hang on a minute, it was his fault, hang on a minute she is putting me down because… she is protecting herself.' You have never done that until today."

In agreement my client said: "Mmmmm no."

Me: "So you have not had an external view of reality, you have had an internal view which is not healthy because then you start getting anxious." Raising my tone to a positive tone I continued, "So any anxiety you feel, realise it is not real… No one had broken your arm…. No one has given you HIV… No one has given you cancer…. No one has punched you in the face… that is real. Anxiety is a state of mind. Change that state of mind by focusing your mind somewhere else. And think – 'You know what, I am right… my kids want a relationship with me…' The kids don't even want your mother there, their Grandma. They are not interested. So what is the real situation….? Focus on the positivity of it. Your kids want you there… they want a relationship with you. Not interested with your mother…."

Dear student, throughout my last dialog that I had spoken to my client, my client had repeatedly agreed with me by nodding her head and saying, "Mmmmm." I hadn't written all of them in as they were many in number.

Please note that I had said to my client, "I am not going to use hypnosis today..." Clearly I had been referring to a deep hypnotic induction. Even though I had said that, I had clearly still used hypnosis with use of a light trance, but my client doesn't need to know all the details of what and why, or how I conduct therapy.

My client then said with true meaning and gratitude: "Thank you! "
Me: "Your dad was wrong."
Client: "Mmmmm."
Talking with regards to my dad so that my client once again knows we are relatable, I said: "My dad was wrong... My dad would always put me down... Nothing, nothing! was good enough throughout my childhood no matter what I achieved.... It was not good enough." Then raising my voice as if angry, I spoke as my dad when saying, "You can do better! It's not good enough that..."
Client: "Mmmmm."
Speaking as myself: "Now you can allow it to crumble you.... Or you can look at it from an external reality instead of just an internal.... External and think – 'You know what... he is wrong. I am just a child.' You was a child. So how can you be wrong? He is the older adult.—"
Client: "Mmmmm."
Me: "He should have taken more responsibility and realised... he needed to go to hospital. His fault."
Client: "Mmmmm."
Me: "And you have got to be harsh and say, 'Tough, what happened was tough' but it was his fault.
Client: "And not mine." (Fantastic led response from my client)
Me: "Not mine (mirroring). So why... drink yourself to death... Why kill yourself with drink? No one has ever survived drink. Ever!"
Client: "Mmmmm."
Reminding my client of the consequences of drinking alcohol I said: "You continue to drink and your body cannot survive... it is impossible... You are going to die... that liquid is death... (Negative association to the drink anchor) Right, you need to start... I want you to start having vitamin pills."
Client: "Mmmmm."
Me: "I want you to eat two banana's a day."
Client: "Okay."

Me: "Bananas are incredible... Banana's fill you full of minerals, vitamins and change the chemical balance of the brain. Are you on anti-depressant pills?"

Client: "Yeah I am."

Me: "A banana.... is better for depression than any pill. Those pills have side effects. I am not a doctor... I can't tell you what to do, but I am strongly advising you to come off those pills. Have you ever had any benefit from those pills?"

Client: "They help me sleep."

Me: "So does relaxation.... So does talking to yourself with self-hypnosis. Your perception of the pill is wrong. You believe it is helping you to sleep but it is a placebo. A banana is brilliant... at sleep. A banana has got natural proteins and chemicals in it that... Change the chemical balance of the brain to make you more positive."

Client: "Mmmmm."

Me: "So what is in that pill chemically.... A banana has it naturally. Two banana's a day every day."

Client: "Yeah."

Me: "Right. When was the last time you ate a banana?"

Client: "Erm I actually had one this morning. I had a banana and an apple."

Me: "Good well it is very important that you eat bananas. Start having vitamin pills because your body—that alcohol dehydrates you and takes any nutrients out of your body and you start to shake. You can start to lose feeling in your hands... numbness. Have you felt any numbness?"

Raising her right hand to show me she said: "Well I do in this hand anyway because I had a very bad break and erm.... I had to have a bone taken out of my hand, and so that hand is always cold."

Dear student, a healed break within a hand, or removed bone does not cause the hand to be cold or shake, so once again her perception is wrong.

Me: "Well cold is lack of circulation."

In a definite high tone of agreement my client said: "Yeah."

Me: "And you can improve that.... by looking after yourself... If your body does not have vitamins it cannot process correctly. It is impossible. Alcohol in your blood stream takes oxygen out of your blood stream, which makes you more lethargic and—"

Client: "Mmmmm."

Me: "You fall to sleep in a stupor. Those pills are not doing you any good at all. Your perception of them that they help you to sleep, they are not at all. It is just your wrong perception of them." Talking in a relaxing monotone I continued, "By sitting there and imagining yourself on a beach. Imagine yourself relaxing on a beach... and just see yourself on that beach. And in your mind see the word 'sleep'. Relax. See a black background with white words saying 'relax' 'sleep' 'drifting deeper and deeper down' 'floating down'. Talk to yourself that way within your mind and that is self-hypnosis. Put some relaxing music on and do that." Changing my tone to normal speech, "You will have more benefit from doing that then a pill... After seven weeks of talking that type of pill, your body becomes immune to it, regardless of the type of pill it is. There was a very interesting documentary on recently and it was about a doctor that took his patients off pills. Anti-depressants. Patients that had diabetes to come off the pills, and he gave them alternatives.... of just going for a walk etc. Depressed people were plunged in to freezing cold water and when they come out of the freezing cold water, they felt euphoric. They felt alive, and it had a bigger benefit than any pill. There were people on pain medication for over twenty years.... Thousands of pounds a year spent on pain medication.... And she [one patient] was on over twenty pills a day. It turned out that her body was immune to the pills after seven weeks of first taking the pills. So for over twenty years she had been taken pills that has zero effect. She was still in pain. You are still depressed but yet you are taking an anti-depressant pill... so what does that tell you?"

Client: "There are two other things.... Going for a walk thing, I have read that in the mindfulness book. Go for a walk around, even if it just around the area that you live and try and look at things in a different way. Smell things, notice things that you might normally walk past two hundred times and never notice. Erm and then the cold water thing I've always done that. I have always... erm... I read it years ago because it suppose too make your hair shinier, and wake you up a bit. And I always like do my shower, you know wash all over and that, and then the last thirty seconds just put it on freezing cold... so I have always done that"

Me: "Yeah it can make you feel euphoric and all of that you know."

Client: "Yeah."

Me: "Erm... Do you believe that you are an intelligent woman?"

Client: "Yes!"

Me: "You are an intelligent woman. There are different levels of intelligence... there is academic intelligence, Maths and English and all of that. Then there is the intelligence of common sense, and of learning. That type of intelligence is far superior.... Than academic intelligence."

Client: "Erm... well at the beginning of this session I wouldn't have said that... but I can tell you know that I am that intelligence." (Another example of my clients changed perception of herself in a positive way).

Me: "Yes you are."

Client: "I have got two degrees whilst working and looking after two children on my own... and I got myself two degrees."

Me: "So you have got the full package... (Boost ego) You have just lacked understanding of yourself a little bit. Now in future— I do phone sessions as well. If you need to talk we can have an hour... at a time on the phone."

Client: "Yeah."

Me: "Right. Which is a lot cheaper... I charge forty five pounds. So if you need to talk... you phone me and talk. You do not turn to alcohol. Alcohol is not a solution to anybody's problem. Alcohol is death (negative association) and that is all that it is. Alcohol is having no relationship with your kids. Alcohol means you stay with your mum for the rest of her life.... Or until you die, and you will probably die before your mum if you drink alcohol... Yeah", I had reinforced several associations of pain to the anchor of alcohol to lead my client before asking, "How is alcohol a solution to anything?"

Client: "... It is not. It is what my subconscious thinks." Great reply from my client as a result of good leadership and due to the simplified way I had educated her.

Me: "Yeah your subconscious is very, very powerful, and it will always overpower your conscious will.... So what you consciously want to achieve in life is irrelevant unless your subconscious agrees with the conscious thought. Those two parts of the mind have got to be friends. You have got to change that movie within your subconscious mind... of what you want. Say positive affirmations to yourself – I am an intelligent woman. I have got two degrees. My kids still want a relationship with me."

Client: "Mmmmm."

Leading my client to see, within her mind, and realise the contrast between her life (positive) and my alcoholic dead friend (negative), I said: "How lucky are you that you are in a position where you can rebuild your life... My friend was in a position where she could not rebuild her life. Nothing, or no one on this earth could help her... She didn't want help. She couldn't rebuild her life. She is dead!"

Client: "Mmmmm."

Me: "Simple as that. Idiot, idiot. You— now other people around her... might feel guilty that she is dead, just like you did with your father. Why should they feel guilty? It was her decision.... She decided to stay in bed with vodka and that. And she committed suicide with vodka. That is what she did. She knew, she wasn't stupid. She had lesion all over her body. When they found her, they found her dead in bed with vodka and whisky bottles around her. And she had lesions all over her body.... Were her body had said, 'Fuckyou'....! No one has ever survived alcoholic poisoning... long-term."

Client: "Mmmmm."

Dear student, have you noticed the subliminal message of indirectly name calling my client an idiot in reference to drinking? And the way I had led, within my client's subconscious, a relatable connection between my dead friends situation, and my client's own alcoholism of self-abuse?

Allow me to explain: In reference to my dead friend with regards to her alcohol abuse, and death, I had said, "She didn't want help. She couldn't rebuild her life. She is dead!" That got my client thinking thoughts of neurological pain, and then I had continued by saying, "Simple as that. Idiot, idiot." I had then associated my client to what I had said by saying, "You—" in reference to my client. By doing so my client was led to make the connection between my dead friend, and her own self-abuse as being the same. The thought was led due to the influenced thought technique, so she realised, without being directly told, that she too is an idiot, the same as my dead friend, with regards to alcohol, and the outcome could also lead to her own death. That was achieved without directly telling my client. I had not directly dictated to my client, I had instead led her to believe that it was her idea (influential thought technique) that she has been an idiot with regards to drink, and that she too could die as a result.

I had then reverted back to referring to my dead friend when saying, "now other people around her..." I had then, as a relatable connection for my client, said, "might feel guilty that she is dead, just like you did with your father." This led my client to make a stronger connection between my dead friend's situation and her own. This in turn further affected her on an emotional, and very powerful subconscious level that leads to positive change.

This indirect influential way of conducting therapy has a greater impact on my client. This is because the led connection, and thoughts, affected her on a powerful, personal, and emotional subconscious level as her own thoughts of an aversion to drinking alcohol

The whole sentence was said as, ""Simple as that. Idiot, idiot. You— now other people around her... might feel guilty that she is dead, just like you did with your father.

Dear student, remember that much earlier in the session I had said to my client, "At what point... is your liver, your body going to say.... Fuckyou! I can't cope with this anymore. It has already sent you signals hasn't it?" As a result of having previously said that, my client had already been led to relate to her body as saying 'Fuckyou' due to her self-abuse from alcohol. As such to compound, within my clients subconscious, a relatable connection between my dead friend and my clients situation, I had continued to talk about my dead friends death, as a result of alcohol abuse, before saying, "Were her body had said, 'Fuckyou'....! No one has ever survived alcoholic poisoning... long-term." The powerful term of 'Fuckyou', said from an abused body, had been referenced to my client previously, and now my dead friend. As such my client was, once again led to realise that she had been going down the same path in life as my friend, where her body also says, 'Fuckyou' in which could also lead towards death. Again all achieved without being direct to my client in order to allow her to believe that the connection made between her life and that of my dead friends, was her idea. I had affected her subconsciously which as you know has a greater, more powerful impact on changing a person's behaviour. Let us now continue with this client case study sessions dialog.

Starting to end the session I said: "Right, give your bother Ken a ring."
Client: "I would do but I realise that as soon as he left that I had left my phone in his car."

Dear student, I stood up to look out of the window and I saw my client's good brother sat in his car waiting. I indicated for him to come on in and he did so. He sat down next to his sister and I explained to them both that I wanted to talk to them together. Both were happy for me to do so.

Talking to Ken I said: "So you made the booking did you?" Of course I already knew that he had, so this was a 'Yes Set Question' to gain compliance and rapport from agreement.

Ken: "Yeah I've just got your book. Basically I use it for self-help myself as such."

Me: "Yeah."

Ken: "And I was looking at it, and it's made me happy anyway, and it was like oh....."

To provoke a reactivated association of positivity, I asked: "In what way has it helped you?"

Ken: "Erm well basically it has changed my outlook on things that are going on and how...."

I finished off Ken's sentence to compound rapport by saying: "It has changed your perception of reality?"

Mirroring me Ken said: "It has changed my perception of reality and basically how things happen. Happen and you know there is nothing you can do about—you can either go with the flow, or you can look at it in different ways. Calm yourself a lot down."

Me: "If you can't change a situation... then you change your perception of the situation."

Ken: "Of the situation." Was said at the same time that I had said the same words, which proved that Ken had understood what he had previously read in my volume one book. And also that he had a very strong rapport with me.

Me: "And then you will always be happy. If your perception of a given situation was wrong and negative, change it." I then looked at my client and said, "Right so... On a scale of one to one hundred.... how beneficial.... was it for you today, with what we have talked about, and the session as a whole?"

Client: "One hundred."

Mirroring I said: "One hundred."

Client: "One hundred percent."

Me: "Good... fantastic. Now think that your other brother [Martin] didn't want you to come... But Ken cares about you—"

Client: "Mmmmm, Mmmmm." Said whilst nodding her head, and looking pleasantly emotional with gratitude towards Ken.

Me: "You are here and you have benefited from it... I am glad you come [came]."

Client: "I am glad I come [came]."

Me: "Good!"

Client: "Yeah."

Me: "That is positive..." I then asked them both, "Right any questions?"

Ken: "I have not got any no." he then said, with reference to his sister, "Well you have got a smile on your face which is good."

Me: "Yeah. Changes her perception of reality."

Ken: "Yeah."

Me: "Her perception of reality was wrong... and she has now changed her perception of reality. If you have an internal view of reality.... you never see the full external... view of reality."

Ken: "Yeah."

Me: "You only see the internal view of yourself. You start to feel sorry for yourself. And if somebody says something negative, then you take it literally as fact, but you don't realise that all they are doing is projecting their pain. It is their issue. If someone comes over to me in a bar and says: 'You fucking ugly bastard get out of my way', Then fantastic, reverse psychology [they mean the opposite]."

Excitedly in agreement Ken responded: "Yeah."

Me: "If they genuinely believe that then they wouldn't have said it to a total stranger. All they are doing is projecting their issues. They have looked at me and thought – 'He has got something that I want'. So they have to slag you off.... to make themselves feel better. Your mother has not got a good relationship with your kids so she has to slag you off... to make herself feel better about her insecurity... That is her insecurity. That is her issue. Now you can either let that bother you, or realise.... pity her. That is her problem. Anybody that puts you down in life. It is just a projection of their own negativity."

My client then waved an imaginary wand and said: ""Expelliarmus!" said because that is her good feeling anchor to the negativity of her mother and brother Martin.

Me: "Yeah! Its nothing to do with you is it?" (No Set Question)

Client: "No."

Me: "It is their issue... So that is an external view of reality in understanding that instead of having an internal view of taking what they say literally, and allowing it to bother you. And why should somebody else ever bother anybody. Nothing anybody can say ever bothers me." To relate to my clients past way of thinking I said, "Use too but once you learn... you think – 'Well that is their issue.' It is not yours."

Smiling my client said: "Mmmmm."

Me: "They can say you are ugly, you're fat, you are this or that... and it doesn't matter. That is there issue..... Harry Potter." I said as I waved my imaginary wand. I then laughed as my client smiled and then I said, "It is amazing isn't it?

Client: "Mmmmm Yeah."

Me: "You could suffer for one hundred years... and somebody could suffer for five years and both people will recover in the same amount of time... because the anxiety was never real. The perception of it was not real then they can start to recover in one day. And from that day forwards it gets better. So from this day forwards.... is the beginning... of your new life. And the past is the past, it is irrelevant. The past is the past, it is there to gleam lessons. You learn from the past, but if you focus on the past.... then you will always live in the past. But by learning lessons from the past... to move forward in a different perception of reality... then you will always be happy. And always set realistic goals..... of what you want to achieve in life. And you can never fail when it is you setting the goals. But if you allow yourself to be bother by somebody else's perception of you.... then you can never be happy.... Are you with me?"

Client: "Yeah!"

I could see that my client was very interested in what I had been saying, so I fed that observation back by saying: "Interesting"

Client: "Yep! Very"

Me: "I am glad that you have brought her Ken. You are a good man.... You are there for your sister."

Client: "Brilliant!"

Ken: "I am always going to be here for her, and other people do care about her."

Me: "Yeah. She has just been focusing on the wrong people."

Ken: "Yeah."

Talking to my client I said: "You need to focus on the right people..." I then focused my attention on Ken when saying, "And you are one of those people." Then talking to my client I said, "And aren't you lucky?"

Client: "Yeah."

Me: "Because that person I told you about had nobody [my dead friend], not one person.... " I didn't finish off that sentence to provoke self-talk in remember what had been said previously. I then continued, "And that is why she is dead.....! You have got a chance of life.... by focusing on Darren and Ken mainly and your kids. Well there you go, I am happy!"

Mirroring me my client said: "I am happy

Ken: "Good, good!"

Me: "I have enjoyed that...."

Dear student, Ken then paid for the session and my client looked at him and said: "I'm going to pay you back. I am being positive." My client then thanked me, and gave me a hug. It is on rare occasion that I allow a client to hug me due to me wanting to end the transference. However on this occasion it was not a confused emotional response of love from my client, she simply wanted, and needed to express her gratitude, and relief that she had been saved. As such I embraced the hug.

Days after this session I received a text from this client which read as follows: 'Still feeling really positive from our session, thank you. X. Looking at a flat this weekend, belongs to a friend of a friend. Fingers crossed!! X.'

I replied: 'Fantastic. Onwards and upwards.'

I later received another text: 'First time in nearly 2 yrs. I actually went & had my hair done at a salon, had mini manicure too! Doing stuff for me!! X'

Two weeks after the session I received an email from her brother to tell me that she is fine at the moment so thank you.

More weeks passed and then I received a text from my client asking for another session, and she was telling me that she had had a bit of a meltdown. She explained that she had cried, and that she never cries. She wrongly believed that it was a sign of weakness, and she didn't like people seeing her as vulnerable.

Dear student, as you know from reading my books, crying is a release of previous suppressed built up emotion. This release is normal and healthy. My client had shown no emotion for years in her warped past version of reality. In contrast she had now rationalised her past, and by doing so she had realised the pain that alcohol had caused her in her life and others, hence the crying. This is fantastic news, but my client doesn't realise this fact.

The fact is she had been vulnerable to abuse and alcohol for years, but yet in her mind it was only now that people had seen her as vulnerable. How wrong she is and as such another session is needed. To date this client has not come for another session. However she continues to text me to assure me that she hasn't touched any alcohol. She text me one night to tell me she was angry because a woman had taken her young son out. She knew the woman but it was causing her a lot of anxiety. I gave her an opportunity to talk with me over the phone, or book a session, but to date she hasn't. I can only help those that know they need help, I can't force a person to seek help.

In later editions of this book I would like to update the progress of this client in the event of further sessions and communications from her.

Testing your Understanding of the Knowledge

DEAR STUDENT, have you ever wondered why most people's minds focus on the repetition of a negative thought instead of the repetition of a positive thought. I am sure you have given that some thought at some point. As such my question to you is this – Do you know why most people's minds focus on a negative thought from their past, or a possible imagined negative future event that causes them anxiety, instead of focusing on a healthy repetitive positive thought that brings pleasure? We all have pleasurable events happen in our lives, but yet the mind still focuses on the negativity in most people's cases. Why is that? Think about that. You should, if you have read and understood my books, know the answer.

It is not as simple an answer to just say the reason why is because they lack control and understanding of their subconscious mind. Of course that is partly why they continue to suffer from negative thoughts, however that is not the reason why they focus on negativity in the first place. So why do people, most of the time punish themselves with repeated negative thoughts instead of repeated pleasure from positive thoughts? You could say it is just a negative habit, but that doesn't answer my question as to why. Mmmmm that's got you thinking hasn't it. Give it some thought before reading on.

Dear student, yes please stop reading and think as to why? As I have stated, it not because it's just a habit. It is not just because they lack self-control, or the lack of understanding of their subconscious, and it's not just because they lack the knowledge of how to change their perception of reality to a positive one. Those points are valid but they are just part of the problem and not the main reason as to why. So what is the main reason as to why people focus on negativity as opposed to the healthier option of positivity?

The answer is very simple and is this..... Remember that the subconscious protects us from potential danger. Whether the danger is real or imagined, it is still an individual's person's perception of their reality. As such the negative thought is real to them even if it is a false-truth. That is why the negative though is repeated in order to protect the person from a possible potential danger. The subconscious is led to believe that it is doing the person a favour by repeating the negative thought. As a consequence of the negative repeated thought, the persons subconscious thinks that it has helped them to be free from real danger, or alerted them to the danger so that it can avoided. And that answers the question as to why people focus on negative thoughts. It is self-protect even if the danger isn't real.

To stop this the person needs to be educated on the knowledge of the mind model, so they need to understand what a habit is, what reality is and how to control the subconscious for self-control. Then they can overcome the negative thought. The subconscious doesn't repeat a positive thought because there is no need to protect the person from the subject of the thought. This is because there is no potential danger in positive thoughts. Fascinating! What seemed a difficult question to answer was in fact simple wasn't it?

I have explained in detail in early volumes of how to overcome the negative with use of creative visualisation, anchoring etc. Change the negative association of neurological pain to the anchor to a humorous positive one, or one of positive control over it. With that being said there is another way. This is a very powerful technique. If the negative thought is not wanted, then you can guide your subconscious to suppress the negative thought by simply stopping thinking about it. Easier said than done you maybe thinking, well no, because it is in fact very easy. How is that done? When the negative thought enters your mind, simply occupy your subconscious onto a different stimulus to distract it from the negative. For example: sing, hum, or say positive affirmations to yourself. Of course this doesn't need to be done out aloud because your subconscious doesn't know the different between verbalising aloud, or within your mind. Both ways still effect you the same on an emotional level which in turn affects your emotions and behaviour. This allows you to make more logical conscious decisions in life. This way in a short space of time the subconscious realises that there is no danger in the present time, and so the negative response of anxiety to the irrational thought is forgotten. Do as advised and I promise you that your mind will focus on the positive a large percentage of the time. This suppression technique of the negative must only be done if no real danger exists. Remember that a small amount of anxiety from the 'Fight or Flight Response', which is 'Acute stress', is very healthy as it drives us to succeed, and does protect us from real dangers if present. However this is only healthy as long as you don't allow the anxiety to overwhelm you to become 'Chronic stress'.

Seven Important Mind Rules and Mind Model

FOR THOSE STUDENTS that have not read 'Volume One'. I have added this chapter due to the importance of learning the whole mind model which includes these seven mind rules.

Most people wrongly believe that the mind and body are two separate things, but the brain is part of the body as a whole, and the mind is part of the brain. You are one being, so the mind and body are the same whole, because they are connected. As such the mind affects you physically and your physical actions affect the mind because once again they are as one connected.

One: Ideas or thoughts result in physical immediate emotional reactions - Thought processes affect the reactions of your immediate behaviour, even if you are not consciously aware of your reaction. For example, a micro-signal in the facial area of looking upset. Negative thoughts of any kind develop instantly into negative, physical, emotional changes within the body. Example: blushing, or imagining being upset, or crying in a certain situation, will result in you doing so, by just the thought of being confronted by that situation. If you imagine a spider is going to hurt you, then the imagined idea causes a physical, emotional, negative reaction to fear, even though the spider is of no danger to you and may not even be there. Thoughts that release powerful emotions, whether real or imagined will, without fail, seep into subconscious mind. Physical, emotional reactions then occur, due to the subconscious accepting the negative thoughts as fact. This is due to the subconscious mind not knowing the difference between what is real or imagined. Of course happy thoughts also have an instant effect on your emotions, and obviously your body as well, by having a positive effect on the body unlike negative thoughts. Consider the mind and body as being the same thing, because the mind is part of the body, thus whatever thought you have, affects every living cell within your body, either negatively or positively, depending on your thought, so it's best to think positively.

Two: The subconscious mind delivers what we focus on - When wanting to achieve a realistic goal that you are not already doing, if you focus your subconscious mind on a negative, then a negative result is what will be achieved and the goal is failed. Alternatively, by playing a positive movie of achieving that same goal within your imagination, then you will achieve that goal on a conscious level, because your subconscious mind believes you have already achieved it, and that makes it easier to do so via the subconscious auto pilot. The reason the subconscious believes you have already achieved the goal, is because you played the positive movie of doing so, and the subconscious mind does not know the difference between what is real or imagined, because both are your reality. You made a conscious decision to do something, your subconscious then plays a positive movie of what you consciously want to achieve, and by doing so, it makes a task easier to achieve, due to the two parts of the mind working in agreement, instead of being in conflict.

What I have just written above, is in relation to a person that wants to achieve a goal that they should be doing, but are not doing it. However, a person with a bad habit is the opposite, because they are already doing something that they should not be doing, so the focus of the subconscious mind has to be different. A person with a bad habit wrongly focuses the subconscious mind with the association of pleasure to the habit, this positive association must be changed to a negative focused association, in order to stop the bad habit.

We are often asked, "Who are you?" The simple answer is to tell the questioner your name. But by doing so, your name does not really tell them who you are. The real answer is, "I am what I focus my subconscious mind on."

Three: Repeated negative or positive focused thoughts result in long-term organic change over-time - When ill, negative, repeated, focused thoughts you have about yourself delay the healing process, and can even kill you with stress due to causing heart failure. When positive with uplifting thoughts, we tend to recover faster from illness. This is the mind and body connection being the same thing. A large percentage of human illnesses are functional as opposed to organic, so continued, negative, focused thoughts that you have about yourself, result in long-term, organic, negative change and as a result illness. The term used is 'Psychosomatic' (illness caused by the mind).So, mind rule one and two develops into mind rule three, if the person continues the negative thoughts about them self. People that cause illness through the mind can be classed as neurotic, and the term used for a person that continuously has psychosomatic illness is a hypochondriac. Even though some people have genuine diseases, negative, repeated, focused thoughts will still result in further negative long-term organic change over-time. With the use of hypnosis, the effect from the negative, focused thought can be changed, by changing the thought to positive. Be that as it may, a negative thought can also result in positive, organic change. For example: a negative thought towards the bad habit of smoking, means the organic change is better for long-term health due to my client avoiding smoking. Of course positive focused thoughts result in long-term positive health benefits for the mind and body.

Four: Imagination overpowers knowledge within in the mind - A smoker has the conscious knowledge that smoking is killing them, but yet they have not imagined the negative effects within the subconscious mind. The subconscious mind is to that end still playing a positive, imagined, associated movie toward the bad habit, and therefore the person does not change, because imagination has overpowered their knowledge, even though the positive association to the habit is wrong and is killing them. Once again remember that imagination (subconscious mind), is more powerful than knowledge (conscious mind), and the subconscious always wins, even when wrong. In order to do anything in life, you have to first imagine doing it, hence why imagination (subconscious mind), is more powerful than knowledge (conscious mind), within the whole mind. This is why people fail, they have made a conscious decision for change, and then tried to consciously succeed, but it is impossible to consciously stop smoking, lose weight, or any bad habit, when the subconscious is still playing a positive movie towards the bad habit. Change the positive to a negative within the subconscious and the bad habit is avoided.

With regards to people with depression, anxiety, stress, low confidence etc, the movie within their subconscious is of wrongly believing an imagined, negative thought as fact. Example: a person may imagine that it is fact that they are useless, ugly etc, so they feel depressed and fear, even though they are wrong, but the negative, imagined thought is fact in their warped perception of reality. Change the imagined thought to agree with logic knowledge, and the person's reality changes for the positive and the problem is solved.

Five: Fixed thoughts can only be replaced by another via the subconscious - If every morning at 7am I got up and consciously made the decision to tap my head three times with my hand, the subconscious, eventually through repetition, takes the task on as a habit, it has become a fixed thought and it is incorporated into my morning ritual. This habit would then be protected by the subconscious. So to get up one morning and consciously force myself not to tap my head, would result in an overwhelming urge of anxiety, as if something is wrong, as if there is a potential danger. This anxiety of feeling there is a danger, is simply the subconscious mind reminding me to do the habit, and because it wrongly feels it is doing me a favour protecting that habit, by keeping me from harm.

In order to overcome this anxiety, and to stop a potential danger, be it real or not, the subconscious reminds me of the habit, so I tap my head for instant relief from anxiety. In other words there is a subconscious resistance to change because the subconscious mind believes it is doing me a favour, so continues to protect the habit even though it is not healthy to do so. Remember the subconscious does not know the difference between a good or bad habit, it protects it regardless, as if there is a danger not to do so. It is simply an associated link between getting up in the morning and tapping my head that became a habit. In other words, repetition that has become a habit through an associated link. Changing the associated link subconsciously, will bring about permanent results.

For example, imagining myself getting up in the morning and doing press-ups, this would occupy my hands so as not to tap my head, and over-time the press-ups become a new more positive habit. This is why a smoker always wants a cigarette first thing in the morning, due to the association of waking up and smoking, they have never imagined doing something else and not smoking.

Dear student, as far as the subconscious mind is concerned, what is the difference between the habit of smoking and the habit of me tapping my head? Think about that for a moment.

The answer is no difference, because both habits are protected within the subconscious, both create anxiety if not carried out, they are in fact the same. A habit. So now let me ask, what is the difference between smoking and swimming within the subconscious? The answer is they are the same, because both habits are protected, because the subconscious mind does not know the difference between swimming and smoking, both are a habit regardless of them being good or bad. The habit of swimming is protected to stop you from the danger of drowning if you fall in to a river, and the habit of smoking is protected to save you from potential danger that's not real. Your subconscious doesn't know there is no danger by not smoking, because the smoker has never told the subconscious mind of the danger of doing the habit in the first place. They have associated pleasure to it, so of course they keep smoking. The fixed thought that needs to be changed, needs to be replaced via the subconscious, because that is where the habit is stored, and not in the conscious mind, so of course consciously wanting to change will always result in failure, due to mind rule four: 'Imagination overpowers knowledge within in the mind', and a combination of the other mind rules. You are starting to see how these seven mind rules are all connected, and of course they are, because we only have one mind each.

Six: Opposing ideas cannot be held at the same time - This means that once the subconscious has accepted an idea as fact, then any opposing conscious ideas will always be rejected. The subconscious, always conflicts against an opposing idea from the conscious mind, and as you know the subconscious is the stronger part of the mind and thereupon, overpowers the opposing conscious idea or thought. That is true unless you change an idea on a subconscious level so that both parts of the mind are in agreement. For example: a person consciously thinks 'I want to stop smoking', but they continue to smoke because their subconscious is protecting the habit and positive associated links of smoking, due to them not showing their subconscious any differently. Remember mind rule four: 'Imagination overpowers knowledge within in the mind', which means the subconscious overpowers the conscious, and that of course has a detrimental effect on a person's life, and that is why, in order to change, it has to be done subconsciously first, to then be a conscious act. Also the subconscious cannot have two opposing ideas at the same time, for example: it cannot think fact (real) and fiction (not real), towards an idea at the same time, it is one or the other idea. The same with the conscious mind, you cannot logically think something is true and false at the same time. Nonetheless as you now know, the conscious can try to oppose an idea from the subconscious, but again, two opposing ideas cannot be held at the same time, so the stronger more powerful subconscious wins.

Seven: Conscious effort alone, results in opposite subconscious success - Conscious effort alone, results in opposite, subconscious success, means that; if you only consciously attempt to try and achieve your goal, you will fail every time. For example: a weight loss client consciously thinks, 'I don't want that chocolate bar because I don't need it'. They have, by doing so, implanted within the subconscious mind, an image of them wanting it and eating it, the exact opposite of the conscious thought. So my client then eats the chocolate due to the powerful suggestion of the image in their subconscious mind of doing so. If you say to yourself consciously: "Don't think of a black cat", then subconsciously you have thought of one, the opposite of what you wanted to achieve. This is why conscious effort alone will never work to overcome a problem, and as you now know, the subconscious is more powerful than the conscious, and it overpowers the conscious will every time. This is why hypnosis is so successful in helping people overcome any problem.

As a student you must learn the mind model and memorise it, so once again here it is.

Three parts of the whole mind:

1) Conscious Mind Functions: Rational logical thought - Makes decisions but the subconscious determines on whether those decisions are carried out or not - One task at once - Willpower - General speech.

2) Subconscious Mind Functions: Many tasks at once - Memories - Imagination - Emotions - Habits - Protects us - In control - Intelligence - Perception of reality - Habitual speech.
3) Analytical or Critical Area: This part of the mind is the conduit connection between the conscious and subconscious, passing information between the two main parts of the whole mind. It is the

part of the mind that reasons to determine new information as being fact or fiction (real or fake), based on information from the subconscious memories.

The subconscious four reference points:

A) The subconscious mind does not know the difference between what is real or imagined.

B) The subconscious also does not know the difference between good habits, or bad habits, a habit is a habit through repetition regardless.

C) The subconscious has no concept of time, past, present or future with regards to associated links.

D) The subconscious also works via associated links which are memories, cognitive thought (Fact or fiction, real or fake, true or false-truth) and emotions (Pain or pleasure) that are associated (Connected) within the mind to an anchor, which can be any sound, touch, taste, smell, or seeing a certain person (Or behaviour), colour, object or place.

The End of another Volume

DEAR STUDENT, if you have any questions you want answering to further your knowledge, or you want a private phone therapy session, then please phone me. Phone calls are free via Wi-Fi on WhatsApp from anywhere in the World. Telephone: 07973481786

Of course I have to charge for my time. Those charges being £25 for half hour or less. Or £45 for over half an hour to an hour. We can cover many topics in that time. Payment must be made before the call is made in order to schedule a time and date for our conversation or phone session. Simply email me some times, preferred length of phone session and dates that are convenient for you and I will book you in.

Email: david.glenn.psychotherapy@gmail.com

In reply to your email I shall send you a PayPal request for payment, or alternatively you can pay via a bank transfer. Let me know your preferred payment method within your email.

I also conduct therapy sessions in person. I charge £95 for a full one and a half hour session.

Dear student, I am writing more volumes, with each being a different client case study, on a different issues. Those issues being gambling, weight loss, confidence issues, low self-esteem, stress, alcoholism, Dysmorphia, paranoia, Obsessive Compulsive Disorder (OCD) and client case studies of people with multiple issues.

What is going to be interesting, when reading more volumes is noticing how I adapt the way I talk to different clients, because each person is unique. You will have already noticed a different from the volume two client to this client case study. In fact I have pointed out some differences. And as you read new volumes, you will learn more by comparing each case study with another. Learn how I change my approach to therapy depending on my client type, their model of the world, and their reactions to what I say. Learn how I use different techniques, and adapt them depending on the client session type and person.

Our third journey together is close to completion; however the journey never ends because life is a journey and not a destination, and the same can be said for your growing knowledge and skills. If anyone ever says they know it all about any given subject then they are very wrong because there is always more to learn. After years of experience it took me a further three years to write the first edition of the 'Volume One' book, and ten years later I was still adding more information as I also continue to learn from experience, and share it with you.

For those wishing to buy the CD's that are mentioned in this book, they are available on one CD Rom for your computer. It has eleven audio hypnotherapy Mp3's with free copyright, this allows you to make copies on CD to sell to your clients to maximise your profits and to help your clients further. For Stop smoking, Lose weight, Boosting confidence, Stress relief, Improve study habits, Focus of concentration, and Pre-talks. Also an induction backing track with subliminal messages of relaxation is on the CD that you can be played in the back ground as you hypnotise your client. Simple go to www.inspiredhypnotherapy.com and then click on the 'Prices & Online Store' page to buy. You can also contact me through the web site if you wish to have personal training from me.

For those students that have studied this book as part of the Home Study Course. If you wish to take the Diploma exam, then the option to do so is available as shown on my web site:

www.InspiredHypnotherapy.com on page 'Prices & Online Store'. The exam is done in your own free time from the comfort of your own home. You simply email me your answers. Students that pass will receive a Diploma Certificate, the same as shown on the web site.

Please add me on Facebook: 'David Glenn - Psychotherapy NLP CBT Hypnotherapy'.

I am building a community of like-minded people including my past students. I will post information on my new published books, and we can all help one another with questions and answers regarding psychotherapy as a whole.

Dear student, can I please ask for a few moments of your time to leave positive feedback on the site where you invested in this book? Without feedback, my time writing will have been wasted, because few people will invest in the book and I simply want to help people to study, to help others, and also for people to overcome their personal psychological problems. I am assessing the feedback to determine whether a fourth volume is wanted or not. So without feedback for this book there won't be a fourth volume.

Please note that I am not a professional writer. I am a therapist. Even so, I have done my best to write this book to help others and you. So please excuse the odd grammar error or spelling mistake. This book has been written in UK English and not American-English. For that reason many words are spelt differently to what our American friends are used to.

Thank you!

Dear student, I will leave you with these wise words for you to think about.

☐ Your version of reality is determined by the questions you ask, and where you get the answers from, and also how you perceive the answers. Change the questions, and source of the answers and your perception of reality changes. As such there can never be one true reality for all people, because unless we are all in a common reality of agreement then we ask different questions to gain answers from different sources. This means that right or wrong doesn't exist in only one version of a common reality, because in an individuals, or groups reality they are always right which can conflict from other people's perception of what is right. Wrong can only exist in your opposition of another person's, or different common groups perception of reality. Think about that.

Dear student, I wish you all the happiness in the world and good health. Be good to yourself and fellow humans. Until our paths cross again in 'Volume Four', bye for now.

Made in the USA
Coppell, TX
10 January 2022